CONTENTS

WITNESSES

APPENDIXES

U.S. POLICY TOWARD, AND PRESENCE IN, HAITI

HEARINGS

AND

MARKUP

BEFORE THE

COMMITTEE ON FOREIGN AFFAIRS
HOUSE OF REPRESENTATIVES

ONE HUNDRED THIRD CONGRESS

SECOND SESSION

SEPTEMBER 13, 27, AND 28, 1994

Printed for the use of the Committee on Foreign Affairs

U.S. GOVERNMENT PRINTING OFFICE

84–415 CC WASHINGTON : 1994

For sale by the U.S. Government Printing Office
Superintendent of Documents, Congressional Sales Office, Washington, DC 20402
ISBN 0-16-046226-6

COMMITTEE ON FOREIGN AFFAIRS

LEE H. HAMILTON, Indiana, *Chairman*

SAM GEJDENSON, Connecticut
TOM LANTOS, California
ROBERT G. TORRICELLI, New Jersey
HOWARD L. BERMAN, California
GARY L. ACKERMAN, New York
HARRY JOHNSTON, Florida
ELIOT L. ENGEL, New York
ENI F.H. FALEOMAVAEGA, American Samoa
JAMES L. OBERSTAR, Minnesota
CHARLES E. SCHUMER, New York
MATTHEW G. MARTINEZ, California
ROBERT A. BORSKI, Pennsylvania
DONALD M. PAYNE, New Jersey
ROBERT E. ANDREWS, New Jersey
ROBERT MENENDEZ, New Jersey
SHERROD BROWN, Ohio
CYNTHIA A. McKINNEY, Georgia
MARIA CANTWELL, Washington
ALCEE L. HASTINGS, Florida
ERIC FINGERHUT, Ohio
PETER DEUTSCH, Florida
ALBERT RUSSELL WYNN, Maryland
DON EDWARDS, California
FRANK McCLOSKEY, Indiana
THOMAS C. SAWYER, Ohio
LUIS V. GUTIERREZ, Illinois

BENJAMIN A. GILMAN, New York
WILLIAM F. GOODLING, Pennsylvania
JAMES A. LEACH, Iowa
TOBY ROTH, Wisconsin
OLYMPIA J. SNOWE, Maine
HENRY J. HYDE, Illinois
DOUG BEREUTER, Nebraska
CHRISTOPHER H. SMITH, New Jersey
DAN BURTON, Indiana
JAN MEYERS, Kansas
ELTON GALLEGLY, California
ILEANA ROS-LEHTINEN, Florida
CASS BALLENGER, North Carolina
DANA ROHRABACHER, California
DAVID A. LEVY, New York
DONALD A. MANZULLO, Illinois
LINCOLN DIAZ-BALART, Florida
EDWARD R. ROYCE, California

MICHAEL H. VAN DUSEN, *Chief of Staff*
RICHARD J. GARON, *Minority Chief of Staff*
MARA E. RUDMAN, *Legal Counsel*

U.S. POLICY TOWARD, AND PRESENCE IN, HAITI

TUESDAY, SEPTEMBER 13, 1994

HOUSE OF REPRESENTATIVES,
COMMITTEE ON FOREIGN AFFAIRS,
Washington, DC.

The committee met, pursuant to call, at 11:05 a.m., in room 2172, Rayburn House Office Building, Hon. Lee H. Hamilton (chairman) presiding.

Chairman HAMILTON. The House Foreign Affairs Committee will come to order.

[Whereupon the committee proceeded with consideration of miscellaneous bills and resolutions.]

Chairman HAMILTON. Before we go to the next order of business, the chair wants to recognize in the audience our former highly esteemed chairman, Dante Fascell.

Dante, we are delighted to see you here. We certainly welcome you to this room where you have performed with such excellence over a period of many years.

Mr. Gilman.

STATEMENT OF MR. GILMAN

Mr. GILMAN. I want to join you in welcoming our former distinguished chairman. We wish him a happy and healthy retirement.

Mr. Chairman, reviewing the agenda for today's markup session, which deals with several important matters before the committee, I notice that we don't have anything with regard to Haiti. Since that has become such an imminent problem, the Clinton administration seems determined about an invasion, and yet this committee, which does have jurisdiction on foreign affairs matters of the entire House, has yet to hold a full-scale hearing on whether or not we should be sending military personnel against the sovereign state of Haiti.

When Secretary Christopher appeared before us in a hearing last month, I urged the administration to seek congressional approval before undertaking any hostile action in Haiti and he replied only that Congress would be consulted. But even consultations would be limited to the leadership and senior members of the relevant committees. They would fall far short of providing for full and open discussion which is needed with regard to this imminent action.

Mr. Chairman, as you know, I have said several times that the President should seek approval of the Congress before sending any troops into Haiti. But even if he chooses not to seek such approval, at the very least this committee should schedule a day of hearings on this issue. I know it is late in the session, but I believe the administration would welcome the opportunity to make the case which, to my mind, frankly, they have not yet made to the American people.

There is a serious question as to whether vital U.S. national interests are at stake in Haiti. The administration's position seems to be that the use of military force against Haiti is appropriate as a means to restore democracy and redress egregious human rights violations. I don't recall such arguments ever being made before in support of committing our troops to combat abroad.

If the grounds for using military force are undergoing redefinition, then Congress, I say, has an obligation to hear those grounds and to make their views known before the ships and planes are launched. I believe we should schedule a public hearing as quickly as possible to hear from our distinguished Secretary of State and Secretary of Defense on the administration's rationale, before committing an invasion force to Haiti, and to draft legislation that reflects the will of the Congress on this issue.

Mr. Chairman, I stand ready to work with you to organize such an early hearing so that the Congress and the American people can learn exactly what is at stake for our Nation in Haiti.

Thank you, Mr. Chairman.

Mr. GOODLING. Would the gentleman yield?

Chairman HAMILTON. Mr. Goodling.

Mr. GOODLING. Earlier on I was looking at H.R. 4541, and I noticed a line that said it is best to help Africans defuse these problems on their own, and I would suggest the same for Haiti.

Mr. GILMAN. Mr. Chairman, I am pleased to yield to the gentleman from California, Mr. Rohrabacher.

STATEMENT OF MR. ROHRABACHER

Mr. ROHRABACHER. I would like to ask, why is it that the President of the United States has sought guidance and permission from the United Nations, and from many, many other countries and governing bodies around the world in terms of his policy for Haiti, but we haven't bothered to have any type of consultation ourselves, either a hearing or any type of a vote on whether or not the U.S. Government should be invading Haiti? Isn't this one of our jobs as members of the Foreign Affairs Committee and as elected officials?

INTERVENTION SEEN AS U.S. INITIATIVE

Chairman HAMILTON. The question is directed to the ranking member, as I recall?

Mr. ROHRABACHER. Yes, sir.

Mr. GILMAN. Well, I do think we have a responsibility in this, Mr. Rohrabacher, and I think we should be exploring it. The President has indicated that he is reaching out to other countries and we are finding very limited support in the Latin American continent with regard to this issue. The CARICOM nations have committed just a trickle of support for anything of this nature. And for peacekeeping, some 17 countries are talking about less than 1,000 troops for peacekeeping. So it will become primarily a U.S. initiative, and I think if it is a U.S. initiative, let's explore it fully here in the Congress and with the American people.

I don't think there is any urgency that we do it within the next few days. Certainly, we have a little more time to explore the issue in the Congress and to make certain the American people understand.

I would be pleased to yield to the gentleman from New Jersey, Mr. Smith.

STATEMENT OF MR. SMITH

Mr. SMITH. I, too, want to make a strong request to the distinguished chairman and to the administration to appear before this committee so the administration can lay out its rationale for the proposed invasion. My constituents expressed this most recently during a series of six town meetings I had in my district, my mail shows this, and I feel it very strongly personally: the administration feels it need to make its case to the United Nations Security Council and seek explicit approval for the use of force from the United Nations; and then to deny that opportunity to the House of Representatives and the U.S. Senate, I think the priorities are backwards. I would hope this type of endeavor would either be supported or opposed. We should at least be given the opportunity to vote on it.

The gentleman's request is very modest that the Secretary of State, perhaps the Secretary of Defense, appear before this committee so we can have a full understanding of this possible invasion, what it means in terms of commitment of force, what risks would likely be incurred by U.S. forces. I had one man come to a town meeting 2 weeks ago whose son is very likely to be part of the invading force, who said this is nuts. He feels that he is willing to go, his son is willing to go anywhere where the President sends him, but there needs to be a very clear coherent rationale for that. Mr. Chairman, that case has not been made, and I would think that we should have that vote prior to any invasion.

Mr. GILMAN. I am pleased to yield to the gentleman from Illinois, Mr. Hyde.

STATEMENT OF MR. HYDE

Mr. HYDE. I want to join those who abhor the fact that we are apparently not going to get a chance to vote on the invasion of Haiti by U.S. military troops before the fact. I have gone through the historical record of all of the military operations that this country has made, and I find it—I cannot find one where American lives weren't involved, where American interests weren't involved, sometimes more peripherally than others, but they were involved, and this situation where I can see no justification whatsoever.

I carry in my pocket the roll call of the vote on January 1991 on Desert Storm. I carry it because it reminds me how many people support gunboat diplomacy where Haiti is concerned but who abhorred gunboat diplomacy where any other place in the world was involved.

If restoring democracy is what we are about, there are many more places, closer places—Cuba certainly is closer to our shores, it is in our backyard—I think to fail to let this Congress express itself, and we represent the people—each of us represents 580,000 people, and to go ahead with this, and while we avert our eyes and look the other way, reduces us to a state of evisceration. We are potted plants in the classical sense.

We are not involved in a determination on behalf of our constituents as to whether we should take a military action against a sovereign country to restore somebody who may or may not be worth the effort. So I just think we ought to have a chance to say something about it.

Mr. Smith mentioned that the United Nations got a chance to debate this but the U.S. Congress is now in a subordinate position to the United Nations. I know they are trying to make the military subordinate to the United Nations. I know they are trying to make our foreign policy subordinate to the U.N. By failing to permit us to debate this, now Congress is subordinate to the United Nations. I think that is outrageous.

Chairman HAMILTON. Mr. Gilman is recognized for an additional 5 minutes.

Mr. GILMAN. I yield to the gentlelady from Kansas, Mrs. Meyers.

STATEMENT OF MRS. MEYERS

Mrs. MEYERS. Mr. Chairman, I think it has been proved in the past that we have to have a public understanding and support in this country of any kind of military action. Without a congressional debate, we are not going to have that kind of public understanding and support.

I don't know of one serious writer or thinker about Haiti who hasn't been extremely concerned about the fact that if we invade Haiti we are not going to be able to get out. There is not a clear exit for us, because we will have to stay there in order to keep stability and peace and to keep Aristide in power.

I think the American people need to know why we are going, when we can get out. They need to know something of what this is going to cost, not just in dollars, but in lives, and I think they don't know any of this yet. The President clearly has not made his case with the American people, and I think in order to do that he is going to have to make his case with Congress.

Mr. GILMAN. I am pleased to yield to the gentleman from Illinois, Mr. Manzullo.

STATEMENT OF MR. MANZULLO

Mr. MANZULLO. Thank you.

When I look at the calendar, today we are talking about granting waiver programs for visas for nannies at a time when American blood is about to be shed in Haiti. Yet the President is not contacting this body; instead runs off to Belize. I think it is a outrageous. I think it is an absolute outrage that this American Congress is being ignored by a President who has no respect for the House of Representatives, who would rather deal with foreign countries to make some type of alignment and be involved in some kind of a peacekeeping operation in Haiti, when this country has been there between 1917 and World War II.

The issue is the role of the House of Representatives when it is faced with a President that ignores contacting this body when this Nation is about ready to go off to war. We need a resolution. At least we need a debate. If we had debated this instead of the bogus crime bill 2 weeks ago, we would have done more of a service to the people of this country.

STATEMENT OF CHAIRMAN HAMILTON

Chairman HAMILTON. The Chair wants to make an observation. We have a pretty heavy schedule here. I want to get through. I know that this is a very important matter. I have certainly taken note of the fact that you want more consultation or briefings. The Chair has requested those. And I understand the process of consultation began this morning at the White House and will pick up here.

The administration does face a bit of a problem because we are going out for another extended break because of the Jewish holiday this week. But I accept the view that there needs to be much more consultation with the Congress and that includes briefings, and the Chair is going to do everything he can to arrange those as promptly as possible.

On the broader point, let me simply observe that whether you have prior authorization of military action is a constant question in American political history. And I think history will show that the Congress has on occasion granted prior authorization for military action, on occasion we have not. On occasion we have done nothing at all. I don't know that there is anything in the Constitution or in the War Powers Resolution that requires prior authorization.

If we look back over the recent commitment of American forces in Grenada, in Panama, in Somalia, in Rwanda, and now possibly in Haiti, and, of course, the Gulf war, you will see quite a checkered pattern. There isn't any single process that we have observed.

But I take the point made by my colleagues on the Republican side that they want more consultation. I think that is perfectly valid, and more briefings from the administration will soon follow.

Mr. Gedjenson.

CONSULTATION DEBATE

Mr. GEDJENSON. I have always felt that administrations ought to come before Congress, because if a situation works and works quickly, they don't need Congress' approval. If it gets more complicated, it needs to be a shared responsibility.

I think, if memory serves, that there was no prior approval in Grenada. There was no prior approval when our troops were placed in Lebanon. There was no prior approval in Panama. I think those were mistakes.

I think it is important for the administration to come before the Congress. I hope as the parties through the years change back and forth, my colleagues will join me in my view that any administration ought to get prior approval.

Mr. BERMAN. Will the gentleman yield?

I think the idea of briefings and consultation are important. I think it would be instructive. And I was wondering if you might pull up the Congressional Record speeches of, just as a sample, members of this committee on the subject of prior authorization, the role of executive authority, the constitutionality of the War Powers Resolution and the role of Congress, just to match what people are saying now with what they have said in the past about the inherent rights of the Commander in Chief vis-a-vis the power of Congress. I think it would be a reasonable piece of information to produce.

Mr. ROHRABACHER. Would the gentleman yield?

Chairman HAMILTON. Mr. Berman, do you yield—Mr. Gejdenson.

Mr. ROHRABACHER. In the military operations that you cited a moment ago, don't you differentiate between a situation where there is an emergency situation or where secrecy is important, as compared to this situation in Haiti where we have had a President announcing an invasion time and time again.

Mr. GEJDENSON. The Panama situation is probably closer than the Grenada invasion, which was of a critical island over which we now have control. I think Mr. Berman's approach may be the best one to take, looking at a historical analogy here. I said at the beginning of my statement—reclaiming my time—I forget who said this, "it is the hobgoblin of small minds to seek perfect consistency," but I do think it is a better policy for this country, as difficult as it may be for a President to get congressional support.

The point that I was trying to make, and I think the point that Mr. Berman was making, is that we should carry this beyond simply Democrat or Republican kinds of debates, that this is an important policy that we should have no matter which party the President belongs to.

What happens is, if it works quickly, whether the President is a Democrat or Republican, it is fine and everybody applauds. Where there is a longer lasting crisis, you need to have a unified Congress behind you. That is why I think it is important for Presidents to come to Congress.

I would be happy to yield.

Mr. BERMAN. To respond to another point made by Mr. Rohrbacher, it is a very interesting point, if what you are saying is that if the President hides the ball, chooses not to exhaust a series of diplomatic and economic efforts short of war, but hides the ball, undertakes a quick, secret attack, then the constitutional war-making power for the Congress is suspended. It is only when he announces beforehand a series of efforts leading to that possible action that the constitutional powers come into play.

I think it is a very difficult kind of a context in which to argue the case that you are seeking to argue.

Chairman HAMILTON. The Chair has Mr. Hastings and Mr. Bereuter.

Mr. Hastings.

STATEMENT OF MR. HASTINGS

Mr. HASTINGS. I want to assert that I am appalled at many of the members' attitudes with reference to this matter, particularly as it pertains to the actions of President Clinton and the administration. I think they have been extremely forthcoming both to the Congress and to the United States.

Secretary Christopher recently asserted that more than 75 times that either he or other members of the administration put forward efforts to alert Congress as to the circumstances involved in Haiti. I for one as a new Member of Congress, probably not as new as quite some time ago, have heard discussions about Haiti ever since I have been here both in the Committee on Foreign Affairs and in intelligence briefings and in special briefings that this chairman has called in order that all Members of Congress must be fully informed. So I don't know what they are talking about when they say that they don't know what is going on. If anybody here doesn't know what is going on in Haiti, we ought to go home and give it up.

Haiti presents a very difficult situation for us but the Chair, in my view, and I associate with the Chair's remarks regarding the Constitution—the President has responsibility to this Nation, as do we, and it is, in my view, harmful to suggest that there is some kind of blueprint for involvement that is going to come magically from debate from the U.S. Congress.

I find it anathema, as well as a south Florida Congressperson, that persons who know very little about the urgency of the circumstances would be hesitant to involve themselves in voting appropriations that would cover the economic losses of people in Florida. Until such time as we can bring ourselves to fully understand those dynamics, enough of this hypocrisy and let's get on with the business of bipartisanship and supporting this President in things of critical concern to this Nation.

Chairman HAMILTON. Mr. Bereuter.

STATEMENT OF MR. BEREUTER

Mr. BEREUTER. Mr. Chairman, I sympathize with your urgency to move on the business of the day, but we are speaking out on Haiti. There is no foreign policy issue on which I feel more strongly than this one. I think our policy with respect to Haiti is foolhardy.

For the first time in my life, I am ashamed of American foreign policy. We are starving children and the general population in Haiti, and the embargo is not having an impact on what is happening there. People will be living the rest of their lives without full mental capacity because pregnant women and young children are being starved by our policy. Can you imagine how those people feel about the American people today?

It is foolhardy for us to be involved in an invasion in Haiti, and the American people know that. We can talk about consultation with the Congress and about the nuances of the War Powers Act, and the administration can consult with me as long as it wishes, but I am still going to do what I can to represent my constituents and work for the national interest. I will do what I can, limited as it may be, to keep the United States from involving itself in this foolhardy invasion.

This is wrong, it is counterproductive, and we will have great difficulty after the invasion. We will walk in there without any difficulties whatsoever. The problems will come afterwards. We will be there for the long term. It will cost us billions of dollars and a great amount of American funds in the long term.

Almost every thoughtful commentator you can see writing on this subject today realizes and says this is a mistake for the President to invade Haiti. The President's credibility is not the reason why we should be invading Haiti, and I think it is outrageous that we are proceeding in this fashion.

Chairman HAMILTON. Mr. Payne.

STATEMENT OF MR. PAYNE

Mr. PAYNE. Thank you, Mr. Chairman.

I hear all of these outcries about foolhardy policies and starving people. We have had an embargo on Cuba for as long as I can remember and that wasn't started by any Democrat. It is a shame that policy breaks down to Democrat and Republican.

We saw the United States invade Grenada and one of the reasons was we had some students who went to a medical college there and we said we have to protect them. In addition, there was the alleged Communist threat. Tell me how important of a threat it really was—when the British were helping Grenada with their programs and building up the country. In fact they were even assisting the Cubans in building the new airport.

When we went into Panama, no one said a word about that. I supported President Bush. I think it was one of the finest things he did at the end of his career, was to go in with a humanitarian mission to Somalia.

It is a shame that everything becomes so partisan. Any time this President does something, it is criticized on a partisan basis. We don't talk about the successes, what is happening in the Middle East with Syria coming in and the Israel situation becoming better.

We don't talk about the fact that North Korea presently now is not the threat it was as it was several months ago. We don't talk about the breakthrough in Northern Ireland with the IRA and Northern Irish Government officials coming together saying that we ought to sit down and talk about having a better solution to the problems in Northern Ireland. So I think it is demagoguery, hypocrisy.

I think that it is a pity that we have become so partisan. I think that it is the right thing to do and I support the President's policy wholeheartedly.

Chairman HAMILTON. Are there further comments?

Mr. Gilman.

REQUEST FOR HEARING ON HAITI INTERVENTION

Mr. GILMAN. I hope that we would not lose the substance of what I proposed, and that was not just for consultations but to have an actual hearing here in our committee, asking the Secretary of State and whoever else would be in authority to come before us to explain the necessity and to give us the rationale for the military intervention.

Chairman HAMILTON. I have taken notes of the gentleman's comments and I thank you for them.

The chair wants to recognize that we have several distinguished visitors from the House of Commons in London.

I want to say how pleased we are to have you here. We welcome you and hope you have a good visit to the United States.

[Whereupon the committee resumed its consideration of miscellaneous bills and resolutions.]

U.S. POLICY TOWARD, AND PRESENCE IN, HAITI

TUESDAY, SEPTEMBER 27, 1994

HOUSE OF REPRESENTATIVES,
COMMITTEE ON FOREIGN AFFAIRS,
Washington, DC.

The committee met, pursuant to call, at 2:30 p.m. in room 2172, Rayburn House Office Building, Hon. Lee H. Hamilton (chairman) presiding.

Chairman HAMILTON. The Committee on Foreign Affairs will come to order.

Today we meet in open session to hear testimony on U.S. policy toward, and presence in, Haiti. Our witnesses include the Honorable Strobe Talbott, Deputy Secretary of State; the Honorable John M. Deutch, Deputy Secretary of Defense; and Lieutenant General John J. Sheehan, Director for Operations, Joint Chiefs of Staff.

We are delighted to have you.

Mr. Talbott.

STATEMENT OF THE HONORABLE STROBE TALBOTT, DEPUTY SECRETARY, DEPARTMENT OF STATE

Mr. TALBOTT. Thank you, Mr. Chairman.

Deputy Secretary Deutch, General Sheehan and I are glad to have this opportunity to talk with you and your colleagues about where we are now and where we want to go in the process of restoring democracy in Haiti.

Today, Mr. Chairman, is D plus seven. American armed forces have been in Haiti for just over a week. We are 18 days from the deadline for the military regime there to step down.

There have obviously been moments of tension, moments of suspense, even moments of violence and danger. There will be more of at least some of those ingredients in the period ahead. But our assessment of the overall situation, Mr. Chairman, in a single phrase, is "so far, so good."

Our intention, also in a single phrase, is "steady as we go."

I am going to leave it to my colleagues from the Defense Department and the Joint Chiefs of Staff to discuss the security situation on the ground. What I would like to do in the next few minutes is discuss some of the political and diplomatic aspects of our Haiti policy. Specifically, I want to bring you up to date on sanctions, on the process of reestablishing legitimate government in Haiti and on the migrant situation.

Yesterday, President Clinton announced that we will lift all U.S. unilateral sanctions toward Haiti, except those that directly affect the three military leaders and their colleagues.

We will lift the restrictions on commercial air traffic and financial transactions between our two countries as well as the freeze on Haitian assets. We are also urging other nations to lift their sanctions.

This weekend, President Aristide publicly called for the loosening of some of the United Nations sanctions in order to facilitate the arrival of humanitarian aid. In accordance with Security Council Resolutions 917 and 940, U.N. sanctions will be lifted completely as soon as the three military leaders step down and President Aristide returns to Port-au-Prince.

In regard to the political situation in Haiti, there are several reasons for cautious optimism. President Aristide is now making frequent statements over our Radio Democracy, urging the people of Haiti to remain calm and asking them not to do anything to disrupt the peaceful transition. The spirit of reconciliation that Aristide has stressed was demonstrated particularly clearly in his radio address on Sunday, in which he offered his condolences to the families of the 10 attaches who were killed the night before.

President Aristide has also called the Haitian Parliament into special session, and has asked the legislature to make it their first order of business to consider an amnesty law. Passing such an amnesty law will be the quickest way of assuring a peaceful transition to democracy and the best way to ensure that the country moves toward reconciliation.

We are hopeful that both houses of the Parliament will be in session by the end of the week, possibly as early as tomorrow afternoon. We have arranged for those Parliament members who have been living in exile in the United States and Canada to be flown back to Port-au-Prince. They are due to arrive tomorrow morning. Our troops are now in the process of securing the parliamentary office buildings in Port-au-Prince to ensure that the Parliament's deliberations are not disrupted.

Looking a bit further down the road, President Aristide has fully committed himself to working with the United Nations, the Organization of American States and nongovernmental organizations to hold parliamentary elections this fall, consistent with the Haitian constitution.

As you know, Mr. Chairman, President Aristide has also recommitted himself to holding Presidential elections by December 1995 to choose his successor.

In regard to the multinational coalition, I am pleased to tell you that 28 nations have now agreed to take part in this effort. Some contingents have been training in Puerto Rico for several weeks now, and we expect police monitors and other multinational forces to begin arriving in Haiti later this week.

Finally, the most recent piece of good news we have had concerns the Haitian boat migrants to Guantanamo Bay; 221 of those migrants voluntarily returned to their country yesterday, and we expect several hundred more to return today or tomorrow.

Now, I want to turn things over to Deputy Secretary Deutch and General Sheehan.

Chairman HAMILTON. Mr. Deutch.

STATEMENT OF THE HONORABLE JOHN M. DEUTCH, DEPUTY SECRETARY, DEPARTMENT OF DEFENSE

Mr. DEUTCH. Thank you, Mr. Chairman.

Let me make a few remarks about the military mission that we have under way in Haiti today. But first I would like to emphasize, Mr. Chairman, that the enterprise that this country is involved in in Haiti is unique in the fact that it has integrated political and diplomatic efforts with a military mission and with economic assistance in order to bring this effort to a successful conclusion.

I want to make a few remarks about the military mission, and begin by saying what that mission is and to emphasize that it will not be subject to mission creep.

The mission is very simple to state. Simply put, it is to establish a secure environment in Haiti and assist in the transition to a stable government.

We have been heartened by the early success in the mission. It is a unique joint operation involving units of the Army, Navy, Marine and Air Corps, unusual in its jointness with army helicopters flying off of Navy carriers in order to assist in the early insertion of troops into Haiti.

The logistics support has been excellent. There has only been one naval casualty, and then today we learned of a single death of—cause unknown, to an American soldier in Haiti. Admiral Paul David Miller, Lieutenant General Shelton have done an excellent job of planning and executing this operation.

As Strobe Talbott has just described, we are entering into a phase of increased humanitarian aid, a phase where we are improving public services and getting the Parliament of Haiti going.

Secretary Perry and General Shalikashvili were in Haiti on Saturday and determined that the troops there understood what their mission was, had adequate resources to carry out that mission, and a high morale.

I will ask, Mr. Chairman, with your permission, General Sheehan to say a few words after my comments on the state of play in Haiti today.

As you know, Mr. Chairman, the central security issue is Haitian-on-Haitian violence. That is our main concern. While the FADH has been cooperative up to the present in some areas of Haiti, it is dissolving, and it is hardly an ideal instrument to assure civil harmony. There is a mix-of-purpose enthusiasm on that island and we must be ready to deal with incidents as they occur.

U.S. troops will not perform normal police functions, but will patrol and deter, and by that presence and their demeanor, assure calm on the island. U.S. troops will intervene directly when life is at stake, provided that they have adequate means and provided that it is safe for them to do so. And, of course, our troops are ready to deal with large-scale violence, riots or looting that will threaten overall stability on the island.

We have currently some 300 military police on the island that have lots of training on how to regulate crowd control and how to assure calm without getting involved in greater levels of violence. The experience of last Saturday shows that our troops are ready and able to deal with threats. The Haitian military will not soon mess with our U.S. troops. And we must be clear about the fact that while incidents will arise and have to be expected, our troops are prepared to deal with them.

In general, the Haitian people and the crowds have been very supportive of our U.S. presence on the island.

In addition to military preparations, there have been supplemental conversations directly with both Cedras and President Aristide, urging them to restrain people that they can influence. President Aristide has been especially supportive of our efforts in Haiti up to the present.

We are taking steps to reinvigorate the Haitian police and to disarm the populace. In the near term, we must rely on the FADH, but we will augment the FADH with military police patrols and beginning at the end of this week, we hope that the international police monitors will enter Haiti to help us build a civilian and democratic police force.

We have already begun disarming the militia, and we will continue to do so throughout the period that we are in Haiti. Our disarmament efforts include a successful collection of all heavy weapons in the Haitian armed services; and we have begun a buy-back program which cannot be expected to be 100 percent successful, but every weapon turned in is one less weapon that can be aimed as a U.S. soldier or a Haitian civilian.

As Secretary Talbott has mentioned, repatriation of Haitian refugees from Guantanamo is beginning. The international forces that are going to be joining us in Haiti are proceeding to train in Puerto Rico, and reequip, and a battalion of 260 people will be entering Haiti to help in the police monitoring activities.

We plan to begin to remove our forces as soon as possible, and should be doing so beginning early next month. We hope to complete the multinational force phase of this operation within less than 6 months and make a transition to a United Nations mission in Haiti where U.S. participation will be less than 50 percent of troops that are involved.

Mr. Chairman, I would like to conclude by making a few remarks about a legislative time limit. We are concerned in the Department of Defense, both the civilian and military leadership, with setting a specific time limit for the military mission in Haiti. An arbitrary time limit, Mr. Chairman, endangers the military in a variety of ways.

First, it forces our military to complete the mission that has been set for them on a calendar—an arbitrary calendar that has been set, not on the military commander's sense of the situation on the ground and what is the best action to protect our troops.

Secondly, it discourages other nations from participating in our international efforts to bring democracy back to Haiti because it says if the United States is going to check out at a date certain, why should they enter?

Third, establishing a deadline places its own dynamic within Haitian politics, and this date could easily encourage Haitian forces to plan incidents for their own purposes around a particular date.

We believe that Congress setting a date for completion of military actions at the outset to be an extremely bad precedent for the

United States. This issue, in the judgment of the civilian and military leadership of the Department of Defense, goes far beyond Haiti.

Let me conclude, Mr. Chairman, by saying military withdrawal will begin as soon as prudent. We all share the goal of getting out of Haiti as quickly as possible. But important for success of the operation and long-term U.S. credibility is that the President and the military commanders have the flexibility to determine how to complete the mission with the least risk to U.S. forces.

Thank you very much, Mr. Chairman. If it is agreeable with you and members of the committee, I would like to ask General Sheehan to say a few words about the current situation.

Chairman HAMILTON. General Sheehan.

STATEMENT OF LIEUTENANT GENERAL JOHN J. SHEEHAN, USMC, DIRECTOR FOR OPERATIONS, JOINT CHIEFS OF STAFF

General SHEEHAN. Mr. Chairman, I don't have a prepared statement, but I would like to review the task that we have given to General Hugh Shelton, and describe where we are as of this afternoon.

The task that we have given General Shelton is, first, to protect U.S. citizens, the Ambassador and staff that are down there, plus the international presence of the U.N. mission that is in Haiti—first; and second, to help stabilize the security situation and assist in protecting the key Haitian leaders in the public buildings that are down there.

As Secretary Talbott indicated, we are flying 12 of those legislators back. We are providing a safe haven for them in terms of guarding the Parliament. Clearly, we have to have an in extremis hostage capability down there. There are violent elements in the Haitian society, and so we have to have that capability there.

We need to pull together the planning for the international and PVO's and NGO's and the legitimate Government of Haiti that is still down there. We are feeding 1.2 or 1.3 million Haitians every single day. Humanitarian flights have started. We started bringing in the PVO and NGO organizations. There are two flights today. There was a flight every single day this week.

We brought a barge in with 170 containers of food and supplies. We are providing technical assistance, and there are hospitals in Cap-Haitien—they haven't seen bandages for a year, x-ray machines don't work, and the doctors don't have essential supplies. We are providing essential medical assistance.

In addition, General Cedras is being managed by General Shelton. He has agreed, though, to start the disarmament in the various departments in his militias. As the days go on, those weapons are being turned in and they are being accounted for.

You clearly see control on the part of General Shelton exercised through Cedras and Francois. It is a security situation that is improving. The FADH and the police in the Cap-Haitien area have in fact been disarmed by the people of Haiti. They turned their weapons in to the Marines. We have over 700 weapons that were turned in by the people at the police station, so the situation is under control.

The situation is a dynamic that is being managed from a tactical advantage. And this gets to the point that Secretary Deutch has tried to make. If you establish a date certain, clearly you are going to change the dynamic on the ground.

We have the tactical advantage now. We should maintain it through the 30th until we get to the 15th. If you put a date certain, then those elements of the Haitian society that are of a violent nature and have a vested interest in changing that to their interest; they are going to do it by killing Americans, and that will change the dynamic on the ground and change the dynamic here in Congress.

THE U.S. MISSION IN HAITI

Chairman HAMILTON. Thank you very much, gentlemen. We will proceed with questions.

I want to begin with the mission. Secretary Deutch, you defined that mission, as I heard you, as one in which U.S. forces were going to establish a secure environment and assist in the transition to a stable government. That is a very limited mission, as I understand it.

What I would like to do is read off several things and ask you whether or not they fall within your definition of the U.S. military mission there.

Protection of U.S. citizens?

Mr. DEUTCH. Yes.

Chairman HAMILTON. To respond to armed attack?

Mr. DEUTCH. Yes.

Chairman HAMILTON. To maintain essential civic order?

Mr. DEUTCH. Yes.

Chairman HAMILTON. To provide for the departure from power of the de facto authorities?

Mr. DEUTCH. Yes.

Chairman HAMILTON. To protect President Aristide after he returns?

Mr. DEUTCH. Yes.

Chairman HAMILTON. To protect Haitian civilians from attack by the Haitian military and police?

Mr. DEUTCH. Yes.

Chairman HAMILTON. To break up the military?

Mr. DEUTCH. Break up the military over time. We would be reducing the military in an orderly and planned way. I am not sure I would use the verb "break up," but we certainly want to help draw down the military and put together a police and military force appropriate to a democratic country, assist President Aristide in that regard.

Chairman HAMILTON. And to disarm the Haitian population?

Mr. DEUTCH. Partially, yes. We cannot agree—cannot take on the mission nor is the mission there to do it totally. We have a buy-back program that has started this morning. We are disarming the population as best we can through a series of measured steps.

Chairman HAMILTON. You are not going to go sweeping through the country and confiscate every weapon?

Mr. DEUTCH. No, sir, correct.

Chairman HAMILTON. To establish and train a Haitian police force?

Mr. DEUTCH. In cooperation with international authorities and the legitimate Government of Haiti, yes.

Chairman HAMILTON. To repair roads, water, electricity and communication?

Mr. DEUTCH. To a limited degree as part of our economic assistance program and in order to support our military operations, yes.

Chairman HAMILTON. And to set up local governments?

Mr. DEUTCH. No.

RULES OF ENGAGEMENT

Chairman HAMILTON. I was reading an article this morning in one of our newspapers about U.S. policy. You may have seen that article. It emphasized the ambiguous nature of U.S. policy with respect to handling Haitian violence.

What are the rules under which U.S. military forces will intervene?

Mr. DEUTCH. Mr. Chairman, what I would like to do is to say that I think most of the ambiguous discussion has been here in Washington. To the best of my knowledge, and I will ask General Sheehan to address this particularly, the actual rules of engagement which have been issued to the troops have not changed from the very first moment.

So, first of all, let me, if I could, just ask General Sheehan; and then maybe I can come back to an interpretation about which—is what we hear about here in Washington about how these might apply, especially in a situation where a U.S. soldier sees violence, Haitian-on-Haitian violence going forward.

But let me first of all ask General Sheehan to actually describe the rules of engagement that have been promulgated through the military chain of command that have not changed since this was planned.

Chairman HAMILTON. General.

General SHEEHAN. Mr. Chairman, the rules of engagement have not been changed since they were issued on Sunday night when we went from a probable combatant role to an intervention role. The rules of engagement allow for the use of force and self-defense of the U.S. forces.

The policy that was made and let out to the troops was that they would not engage in acts of Haitian-Haitian violence, and that was the policy discussion you were referring to. But the rules of engagement clearly allow for the right of self-defense, the use of proportional force, and when forces perceive that they are in harm's way that that force can be used.

Chairman HAMILTON. Well, if they see one Haitian threatening the life of another Haitian, what do they do?

General SHEEHAN. The graduated policy that was given to the troops is, first off, that they use the existing FADH police that are in place. They encourage them, first off, not to do that.

Second, they find an NCO or an officer, if that is possible, and encourage him to stop doing that. They report it through their chain of command——

Chairman HAMILTON. An American or Haitian?

General SHEEHAN. Haitian. Clearly, the first line of defense is to modify the behavior with the Haitian military. They will report who the individuals are and—et cetera. It is only after they have very quickly gone through these steps that they allow themselves to intervene between Haitian on Haitian violence. You can make that decision in 5 seconds or 3 or 4 minutes, depending on what the situation is.

Chairman HAMILTON. But if they are confronted with a life-threatening situation or large-scale violence, they can intervene?

General SHEEHAN. Yes, sir.

OPPOSITION TO DATE CERTAIN FOR U.S. WITHDRAWAL

Chairman HAMILTON. All right.

I wanted to ask about the date certain. You were very specific as to why we should not include one. Do you think that we raise the risk of injury, casualties to our own forces, if we put in a date certain?

Mr. DEUTCH. Yes, sir.

Chairman HAMILTON. Can you explain that?

Mr. DEUTCH. Well, if the troops have been given certain set missions to accomplish, and they are told that these missions which, under the most careful, thorough planning that I am familiar with in spending 30 years in looking at the Department of Defense, if they say it is going to take a period of months, and they are suddenly told it has to be done in 60 to 90 days, in order to accomplish those missions they are going to take risks. They are going to have to move things faster, move through the countryside faster, go through the towns—and go through the towns and the police and military installations in the towns at a more rapid rate than the planners thought was prudently the best way to go in order to minimize casualties to U.S. troops.

And it is in that particular way that it runs a greater risk for U.S. forces.

I also believe, Mr. Chairman, that it encourages—it encourages extremists in the Haitian community to take advantage of that date, manipulate the political process and the military process, knowing that there is a date certain, planning extreme events around that date certain in order to have the United States, or try to get the United States to move in a manner that is convenient for their political purposes.

Chairman HAMILTON. Mr. Leach.

GEOGRAPHIC RATIONALE FOR INTERVENTION

Mr. LEACH. Thank you, Mr. Chairman. As we all know, there are a lot of problem spots in the world from Rwanda, Bosnia, Burma, whatever. And yet the rationale for this particular intervention, among other things, hinges on that it is close to our shores. So we appear to have a new American doctrine that is reminiscent of the "Roosevelt corollary" to the Monroe Doctrine. But it comes down to a doctrine of geographic propinquity, and that has some very salient implications for U.S. foreign policy.

It also has very profound implications for other countries' foreign policies. Once you establish a doctrine of geographic propinquity, you are suggesting that other countries of the world may have a similar doctrine. We have all known of the Brezhnev Doctrine. How do you think this is going to play out over time?

CUL-DE-SAC NATURE OF HAITI POLICY

Finally let me just note, as a corollary to that question, I have been very convinced that the Haitian diplomacy of the United States, which quite frankly was a very ad hoc action and was saved from a worse catastrophe by the Carter mission, has become of a cul-de-sac nature. A series of decisions were made that, if they didn't work, would lead to military intervention unless the United States chose to backtrack on decisions made.

For example, we put in sanctions that were clearly going to be tough on the people of Haiti; therefore, we had the choice either of pulling off the sanctions, which had created more refugees, or of going in militarily to halt the exodus of boat people.

And so my query here is two things in terms of thoughtfulness: What of this doctrine of geographic propinquity, and secondly, was there a cul-de-sac nature of American foreign policy that ought to be reassessed so that we don't get ourselves in a similar bind in another circumstance at another point in time?

THE GEOGRAPHIC FACTOR

Mr. TALBOTT. Mr. Chairman, let me try to be responsive to Congressman Leach's question. And at some point during the discussion, I would like to come back to the question of the delineation of the mission of the multinational force, which is the current phase and the UNMIH, particularly with regard to the police functions; and so I hope we can have a chance to do that.

Congressman Leach, obviously geography is a factor in any nation's definition of its national interests, not to say its vital national interests. Obviously geography is a factor here. And it isn't just a question of propinquity, of course. It is what comes along with propinquity or geographical proximity.

And in many cases around the world, including this one, the disintegration of a political situation in one country can produce an outflow of refugees who, in various ways, impinge on the interests and capacities and resources of neighboring countries. And we saw that in spectacular and alarming fashion this summer in the case of Haiti.

But I take your point, and of course, we understand that other countries might, looking at this situation, say why shouldn't we be able to define our national interests in the same way? I hope that other countries looking at this case would follow our example in several respects.

First of all, the United States showed immense patience through two administrations, or much of two administrations, in attempting to use every means at our disposal, short of the use of force. That meant political pressure, diplomatic pressure, economic pressure, and sanctions. And it was only when those other means were exhausted that we resorted to the credible threat of the use of force.

INTERNATIONAL SUPPORT FOR U.S. POLICY

The second point I hope other nations observing this case would notice and would apply to themselves would be that the United States scrupulously, assiduously and successfully worked through international bodies and under international law.

We had an unprecedented degree of support within the Organization of American States, and the ultimate resort to force was under United Nations Security Council Resolution, 940. And this is obviously particularly germane today when the President of the Russian Federation is visiting the United States; and the issue of how the great powers of the world are going to define their national interests and peacekeeping in the post-cold war era is very much on the agenda of the discussions between the two Presidents going on right now.

CONGRESSIONAL CONSULTATION

Chairman HAMILTON. Mr. Torricelli.

Mr. TORRICELLI. Thank you, Mr. Chairman.

Mr. Chairman, history may well determine that Haitian democracy has been enhanced by the American occupation, but will almost certainly conclude that democracy in the United States has not been helped. The United States is occupying a foreign government, a foreign country, without this Congress ever having made a judgment and against the overwhelming sentiment of the American people.

The administration has committed this Congress to what will probably be a $1 billion expenditure and almost certainly will involve the loss of life, having placed the honor of the nation also at stake. It may be the right policy or it may be the wrong policy, but by definition in a democratic society, any judgment without the consent of the governed is suspect.

You have—by this action, have influenced my own thinking about our country and our system of government to a great degree, but none more than my already strong feelings about term limitations. Because listening to you, Mr. Deutch, today I saw Mr. Shultz arguing with us against limitations in Lebanon; I was reminded of Mr. Weinberger arguing against putting any restrictions on the contras; Mr. Aspin, in Somalia.

If I could take back any one day of my whole life, no less my public service, it would be when we sat in this chamber and listened Mr. Shultz arguing how there could be no definition of mission, no restrictions on time, on the Lebanon military presence; we couldn't tie the hands of the President.

Mr. Deutch, tying the hands of the President is what shared constitutional responsibilities are all about.

I can remember George Bush meeting with us privately before the Persian Gulf War. He shared all the sentiments of this administration about the constitutional prerogatives of the President, but he made a judgment that the Persian Gulf War could not commence without some intervention by the elected representatives and the support of the American people because it was not right to ask the country to make that sacrifice without knowing that we stood together.

I strongly believe that this Congress must be heard on this question. I am offended that General Cedras, a leader of one of the most reprehensible and despotic governments, would not reach an accord without consulting with the leadership of his Parliament and the de facto President of that regime, but the President of the United States made a judgment about a military occupation of Haiti without this Congress ever reaching a judgment.

There is a chance to reverse this unfortunate precedent and have the leaders of Haiti understand that we stand together. While I disagreed with the decision to enter Haiti, I accept that it has been done. I want it to be achieved successfully, and I want there to be no mistaking in the Haitian military that we do have a common purpose now in seeing it succeed.

THE CASE FOR A DATE CERTAIN

You fundamentally misread the decision of this Congress in reaching a vote on a date certain, that it represented weakness. That is what Mr. Shultz and Mr. Weinberger and Mr. Aspin and those before you have all argued. A vote by this Congress setting a date certain is also an endorsement of a policy. It makes clear that there are not divisions within the U.S. Government. That is a vote of strength.

You have not argued that a date—any particular date is wrong. You have argued that any date would be in error, which suggests to me that a date—setting a deadline in a year or 6 months or 2 years would somehow jeopardize forces. Indeed, the lives of our forces have been used a shield to defend against the sharing of constitutional powers which rests in each institution.

No one is suggesting that if a date is set, it would not be extended. No one is suggesting, because a date is set, that we do not naturally foresee a succession in our role of those of the United Nations force. Indeed, that is exactly what we do contemplate.

The possibility of a congressional resolution is an invitation to the administration to share properly divided constitutional powers and to proceed in this policy together. I would greatly regret if the administration does not accept the invitation to end any division and proceed with the policy together.

CASE FOR DOCTRINE-BASED FOREIGN POLICY

Finally, Mr. Chairman, indulge me for a final second. I share Mr. Leach's concern also about the policy that is evolving. This Nation should not have foreign policy by anecdote; it should be by doctrine. It would appear to me that a doctrine is being established and spheres of influence are being established where there is a right of powerful nations to have economic and military forces determine events in their neighboring nations. Simply because a nation is strong economically or has military power does not mean it has any monopoly on wisdom. It appears to me that it has neocolonialist overtones.

In this instance, the United States is certainly right and the Haitian military is certainly wrong. But since the policy is being determined because of immigration policy, historic relationships, proximity to the United States, I believe you are inviting the question about U.S. response to future coups in Central America or even

South America. You are begging the question about whether Russia or France or other powers do not exercise similar responsibilities in spheres of influence that they would define for themselves.

Indeed, in Rwanda, France has already done so. But, remember, simply because, in Rwanda, France may have been right or, in Haiti, the United States has a superior position to the Haitian military does not mean that the precedents that are being established will not be followed, what clearly is a new and emerging doctrine of the Western powers in the Third World.

So, to conclude, for all of the dangers that invites, they mean nothing; the fact that in the service of Haitian democracy we are compromising an important constitutional principle in American democracy, that we not only are achieving little, but potentially doing great harm to a system of government that is much more important and invites far greater dangers if executive powers in this country are to continue to accumulate and risk a great balance which has been the savior of our own freedom.

Thank you, Mr. Chairman, for indulging me the time.

MILITARY CONSEQUENCES OF CONGRESSIONAL TIME LIMIT

Mr. DEUTCH. Mr. Chairman.

Chairman HAMILTON. Mr. Deutch.

Mr. DEUTCH. I was hoping, Mr. Torricelli, that I could explain that I was not arguing a constitutional principle. I was trying to make a much more limited remark. The limited remark that I was making has to do with the consequences of a military plan to achieve a well-defined mission by setting an arbitrary time limit.

It may be that there are other mechanisms, other mechanisms that can be found to express yours or Congress' view on this or prior military missions that have been undertaken by this country. I was making a narrow remark, which I believe is accurate, and that is the consequence for the military in carrying out a designated mission by putting in a time limit. It is that mechanism for expressing the congressional will that I was addressing.

So I want to assure you that I was not making a big constitutional principle, but trying to explain the consequences for the achievement of a military plan that has been worked out in great detail from setting this particular way of expressing congressional will.

Mr. TORRICELLI. Mr. Chairman, I will respond very briefly. I recognize my time has expired.

Mr. Deutch, we all take the same oath of office to the Constitution. We can differ on whether a time limitation for withdrawal from Haiti has practical difficulties. There should be no debate that it is constitutionally a superior, if not constitutionally required, position.

As the administration balances the practical difficulties of such a limitation with the overriding constitutional advantages, it should be a clear judgment. Adhering to the Constitution will always have some practical difficulties. It may often or always be inconvenient. It is also the better way to govern.

And it would have, in my judgment, been the better policy to come before this Congress, having weighed the two and having reached the proper determination.

Thank you, Mr. Chairman.

THE CASE FOR CONGRESSIONAL AUTHORIZATION

Chairman HAMILTON. Mr. Smith.

Mr. SMITH. Thank you very much, Mr. Chairman. And I want to welcome our distinguished panel. Let me say at the outset, Mr. Chairman, that those of us who have raised serious questions and continue to question the deployment of U.S. forces to Haiti were never concerned about our force's capability, their commitment or professionalism; rather our concerns were exclusively focused on the health and the well-being of our men and women in uniform. To send others into combat or into an extremely hostile situation is the most serious decision that anyone can make.

Thus, I remain deeply concerned as to how our commander in chief has put U.S. forces in danger without first seeking authorization from those who directly represent the families and the individual servicemen and service women. Mr. Chairman, this isn't some petty fight about the legislative branch versus the executive branch. This is not a turf battle. What makes this particularly troubling are the lengths to which the administration went to procure U.N. authorization while bypassing the legitimate representatives of the U.S. citizens, namely the U.S. Congress.

One question—and I do have others I would like to pose as well—why wasn't prior congressional authorization sought? Was it merely a legal or a pragmatic, practical consideration that the votes simply weren't here on the Democratic nor Republican side?

ARISTIDE'S RECORD

The second question I would like to raise, in response to questions that were raised by the Senate Foreign Relations Committee in May of 1993, Assistant Secretary Alex Watson said, and I quote, "There was ample evidence that President Aristide incited intimidating or violent behavior among his followers."

Three days before President Aristide was deposed he was speaking to supporters at the National Palace on September 27, 1991 and said, "If you catch someone who does not deserve to be where he is, do not fail to give him what he deserves. Do not fail to give him what he deserves," he said again.

"What a nice tool. What a nice instrument. What a nice device. It is a pretty one. It is elegant, attractive, splendorous, graceful and dazzling. It smells good. Wherever you go, you feel like smelling it. It is provided by the constitution, which bans Macoutes from the political scene."

And one question: Was President Aristide talking, Mr. Talbott, about necklacing when he said this? If that is the case, and especially in response to what Secretary Watson said, what assurances do we have that Mr. Aristide has changed his means, his methods?

Yes, he was duly elected with a mandate from the people, but he also has a record that cannot be lightly dismissed. What assurances do we have that he has changed his methods? And, I would like to know whether or not, in your opinion, he was referring to necklacing.

IMPACT OF POLITICS ON POLICYMAKING PROCESS

Then, Mr. Chairman, there is the issue of politics. As you know, there was a leaked confidential note for the file dated May 1994, about a meeting between Mr. Dante Caputo and the Foreign Minister of Canada. The Foreign Minister said, "concerning the United States' position such as laid out by Strobe Talbott, Dante Caputo thinks that time is short and that the situation today cannot last beyond July. Dante Caputo emphasizes that Haiti represents a test case for which the United States has to have found a solution before November."

I would like to know for the record, Mr. Talbott, exactly what is the reference to November? Is there anything in that statement that speaks to the November elections? On the record, knowing that what you say is extremely important here, was any of the decisionmaking in any way influenced by the upcoming elections?

LEGALITY OF AGREEMENT

I do have other questions for the second round. But finally, how do you square the assertion that the Carter agreement is legally binding when the de facto—we consider him a persona non grata—President Jonassaint signed the agreement with President Carter? Why is that legally binding when that same person lacked the authority to bring back the Parliament in order to determine whether or not an amnesty ought to go forward?

It seems to me that we have his name on one document and one document only, and that is construed to be authentic and any other act that he has taken prior to or after that is deemed to be lacking any authority. How do we back that up?

Because I do believe, Mr. Chairman, that making sure the signature is binding seems to be an important detail. Also, were we seeking General Cedras' signature and, for reasons that you might want to explain, that was not accomplished and therefore we went to someone else who could then sign the document?

I do have other questions for the second round, and I would appreciate your answers to those.

INTERVENTION CONSISTENT WITH PRESIDENTIAL AUTHORITY

Mr. TALBOTT. Yes, sir, Congressman, on the first point, as the President and other members of his administration, including Secretary of State Christopher made clear many times, President Clinton felt, and continues to feel, that he was operating and is operating completely under the authority as commander in chief given him by the Constitution.

He feels that he has both precedent and the Constitution very much on his side in this important debate which we have joined here today. And he feels that in addition to proceeding in a way that maximized the chances of the success of this operation, he also was upholding a principle of Presidential authority which his predecessors of both parties have asserted and upheld themselves on numerous occasions and, no doubt, that his successors will also uphold.

COALITION SUPPORT FOR INTERVENTION

Let me be very clear on a matter relating to the second point that you raised and that has to do with our working through and with the United Nations.

The United States of America did not go to the United Nations to seek permission to use force, if necessary, in Haiti. The United States would never, under this administration or I suspect under any administration, ask permission of another country or of an international body to do what it considers in the interests of the United States.

Mr. SMITH. Would the gentleman yield on that one point? Had the U.N. Security Council voted no, would we not have had an occupying force there?

Mr. TALBOTT. Had the President determined that it was in the vital interests of the United States to act alone in this instance, the answer is emphatically yes. What the United States did do in this case was go to the United Nations and work through other international bodies as well, notably the OAS, to put together an unprecedented coalition for several reasons. One is so that the leaders in Port-au-Prince would understand that they had the entire world community against them. And we were successful in putting together this coalition.

But a clear distinction should be made on the one hand, assembling a coalition, and on the other hand, seeking the permission of the United Nations or any other body.

ARISTIDE'S RECORD

As to your question about President Aristide and his own record when he was the President—when he was in power as the President of Haiti, there is no question that there was and no doubt will continue to be some controversy about that record.

Several points are germane at this point in the evolution of Haiti's political life. First, I think nobody would contest that President Aristide's human rights record was by an order of magnitude better than that of his predecessors, and better than that of the leaders of the coup who replaced him.

You asked about what President Aristide means when he uses certain phrases. I can only speak with authority to what he seems to mean now when he emphasizes reconciliation. When he counsels his own people and his own followers to avoid revenge. He has been putting out that message consistently over the past months, and particularly in recent days.

He has also convened the Haitian Parliament, which should begin meeting as soon as tomorrow, and he has put as the first order of business, once the Parliament convenes, the passage of an amnesty law, which would be, as it were, the institutionalization of, the legislation of the principle of reconciliation.

The final point I would make in that regard is that from the beginning—and this goes back, I think, to the position of the Bush administration when senior officials of the Bush administration said this coup must not stand. The issue has not been so much one man—though, of course, one man does lead the democratically elected Government of Haiti; the issue has been the restoration of democracy as an institution, as a process, and as a set of principles.

And I think that it was important substantively and symbolically that on the eve of the deployment of the American forces followed by international forces, President Aristide used a meeting at the White House to reassert a commitment that he has made before, and that is that he would serve out his term as stipulated by the Haitian constitution and that he would preside over what we all hope will be a free, fair and peaceful election in December of 1995 and turn over his office to his successor in February of 1996.

TALBOTT-CAPUTO COMMUNICATION

You have asked, Congressman—and you can imagine you are not the first to put this question to me—about certain memoranda supposedly coming from Dante Caputo, who until recently was the special envoy of the United Nations Secretary General to the OAS with regard to Haiti. I simply cannot fathom exactly what was in those memoranda or explain to you everything that allegedly was there; I have not seen the memoranda myself.

But I can speak with absolute authority as to conversations that I had with Mr. Caputo on several cases—several occasions in recent months. And I assure you that, first of all, I never set any kind of deadline for this policy, because the President of the United States had not set such a deadline until much later in the game than when Mr. Caputo and I were seeing each other.

What we talked about was the dynamics of the situation itself, and the dynamics that were driving the situation had to do with the steadily deteriorating human rights and humanitarian situation in Haiti and also, of course, had to do with the attempt to use all necessary diplomatic means, including those in which Mr. Caputo himself was engaged.

But in straightforward answer to your straightforward question, I never discussed with Mr. Caputo, or for that matter with anyone else that I was dealing with during that period, November, in any context—notably, in any context having to do with our domestic elections.

POLICY DRIVEN BY DYNAMICS IN HAITI

Mr. SMITH. Was it discussed within the administration? Was the November election ever an issue within the administration?

Mr. TALBOTT. The issue within the administration, and I think in the public debate as well, was driven by the dynamics in Haiti itself. Nevertheless, I personally, as a participant in the internal as well as public debate, had some sense of urgency, my own sense of urgency had at the end of the time line, the period in which we are now talking—the September timeframe, not the November timeframe—and that has to do as much as anything with such things as the dramatic increase in terror, which was already at a very high level; and also the exhaustion of the diplomatic process that was particularly dramatic, which just before Secretary Deutch and I went down to the region at the beginning of September, when Dante Caputo's last attempt to make an approach to the Cedras regime failed. And that is when the Secretary General of the United Nations said publicly, "Diplomacy has failed here." And that is when we in the international community, led by the United States, decided to make good on the resolution, 940.

Chairman HAMILTON. Mr. Berman.

Mr. SMITH. Mr. Chairman, there were some questions posed that were not answered.

Chairman HAMILTON. Did the witnesses have any further responses?

LEGALITY OF CARTER-JONASSAINT AGREEMENT

Mr. SMITH. The Jonassaint signature and the fact that it was only binding in the one instance with Mr. Carter.

Mr. TALBOTT. I am sorry, I retained almost all, but not all of your questions. As I understand your question it goes in some ways to the nature, in the eyes of international law and perhaps diplomatic history, of the document that was signed by President Carter and the de facto President of Haiti, Mr. Jonassaint.

I hope you will permit me not to plunge into that debate. What I would like to seize upon is the opportunity to say what was important about that agreement, what was operationally important about that agreement. And what was operationally important was that that agreement included a date certain, speaking of date certain, for General Cedras, General Biamby and Colonel Francois to have to leave power; that was a provision in the agreement that was included at the insistence of President Clinton.

And the combination of that date certain and the willingness of the de facto and the military regime down there to cooperate with General Sheehan's colleagues during the interim is what has permitted us to have something that is almost without precedent, and that is, as it were, a permissive invasion, an invasion that has been an intervention that has been carried out with remarkably little violence, as a result of which American and Haitian lives have been saved.

Chairman HAMILTON. Mr. Berman.

TIMETABLE FOR WITHDRAWAL OF U.S. FORCES

Mr. BERMAN. Thank you, Mr. Chairman. I am sorry that I got called to another markup, and I missed the earlier questions. I hope I don't repeat anybody else's points here.

I initially have to say that while I was very skeptical about the invasion and certainly felt that Congress should vote, the way things have worked, I think the administration deserves a great deal of credit for what it has done in Haiti so far, and it is heartening to see the warm welcome our troops received.

I cannot believe that a large number of our colleagues would want to see us turn tail tomorrow and pull out automatically at this particular point, if for nothing else than the message it would send everywhere else in the world.

But in the discussion of an end date or a reauthorization, can you just give me a sense of the timetable that you have? It is not a commitment, it is not an announcement. It is simply a best guess of what it looks like to you now, understanding that things could change.

Mr. TALBOTT. Yes, Mr. Berman, I will be happy to do that; and perhaps with the chairman's permission, I could fold into my answer a point that I wanted to add to something that Secretary Deutch said earlier when talking particularly about our efforts with regard to the police function in Haiti.

It has been our plan all along that the first phase of this operation, the so-called multinational force phase, would last a matter of months—to the end of this year, perhaps to the beginning of next year at the outside. The reason that we had hoped very much to preserve maximum flexibility is, of course, the length of that part of the phase will depend on the conditions on the ground.

TRANSITION TO UNMIH

We are a week into this, and we are encouraged by what we see, and both of my colleagues have spoken to that. If we continue to be encouraged, we would hope, within a matter of months, to be able to hand over this operation to what is called the United Nations Mission in Haiti, UNMIH, U-N-M-I-H. That will be a considerably smaller force totaling about 6,000, no more than half of whom would be Americans and not all of those, military personnel.

If I could make two points here: First, Secretary Deutch mentioned that it is an important part of our overall mission in Haiti to professionalize the military and help the Haitian Government set up a truly civilian police force that is responsive to the legitimate government and to the needs of the people, as opposed to being an instrument of terror, which is what it is now. And it is now basically a part of the armed forces of Haiti.

During the multinational force phase, our purpose is more limited than that. During this initial phase, our purpose is to work with the Aristide government to set up what we are calling an "interim police force," the personnel of which will come entirely from the ranks of Haitians, many of them from the current armed forces.

Their activities, in turn, will be supervised by 500 to 600 international monitors from other countries—that is, not Americans—who will be coming in under various flags as part of the multinational force.

During the second phase, or UNMIH phase, one of the principal purposes will be to deconstruct and reconstruct, you might say, the military and the police force so that they are separate entities. It will be a much smaller military and a more genuine police force.

DANGER OF SETTING TERMINATION DATE

The point I wanted to make with regard to the risks and indeed the dangers that we would run if there were a legislatively or congressionally imposed date certain is this: Under the arrangement that we have with the United Nations, the United Nations is not going to come in with the UNMIH, the United Nations force, unless and until General Sheehan's colleagues on the ground in Haiti certify that the situation is secure and stable and safe.

If we are operating against a congressionally mandated date certain, that would provide a very unwelcome incentive to forces in Haiti, who do not want to see the United Nations mission deployed, to stage a violent provocation of some kind at D minus five, or something like that, if D is the date certain for us having to be out. So we could end up jeopardizing the ability to even have the second phase of this operation, which I think would undercut the mission as a whole.

OPTION FOR REAUTHORIZATION

Mr. BERMAN. Mr. Chairman, may I make one observation?

Chairman HAMILTON. May I interrupt? Mr. Talbott, a date certain doesn't necessarily mean that the Congress is saying U.S. troops have to be out by that date. We can reauthorize. Do you understand that?

Mr. TALBOTT. Mr. Chairman, of course. And I look to the wisdom of this body and to deliberations between this body and the administration during the weeks ahead. But I do think one needs to examine in fairly stark terms the risks associated with a date certain.

Chairman HAMILTON. It is obviously possible that we would require withdrawal at that point, but it doesn't necessarily mean that. We authorize participation up to a certain time; Congress reserves the right from that point on to extend it or not. That is the point.

Mr. TALBOTT. I understand.

Chairman HAMILTON. Excuse me, Mr. Berman.

Mr. BERMAN. If I may make an observation also? It is a little bit along those lines.

I think setting a date certain by which U.S. troops withdraw or you shift from phase one to phase two is nuts. But I do think that a date by which we ask Congress to reconsider whether or not to continue the authorization is not a termination date; it is simply a way by which Congress exercises what we think are our institutional powers and roles—far more sensitively, presumably, than the blunt instrument of denying funding in the middle of something—to participate in this process, to oversee this process.

And even if you don't buy that institutional reason for a date by which we should reauthorize, not a termination date, I think it is a very nice defense against the irresponsible notion that we should immediately withdraw tomorrow.

Mr. TALBOTT. I understand, Mr. Berman. I would only ask that as this issue proceeds to what I am sure will be a good outcome that we all be mindful of the danger that if we are not careful, we could embolden our foes and discourage our friends, including our international friends on this issue.

Chairman HAMILTON. Mrs. Meyers.

MISSION CREEP

Mrs. MEYERS. Thank you, Mr. Chairman. I have three questions, and the first one I will direct to Mr. Deutch because I think it was he that said that we would not have mission creep—or maybe that was Mr. Talbott—where the mission——

Mr. TALBOTT. I will say it, too.

Mrs. MEYERS [continuing]. Where the mission just gradually enlarged. But in an AP story today it said American officials have expressed concern over what they call "mission creep"; which is defined as going to a country with a specific mission, in this case to restore the elected government, but finding their role slowly expanding.

In the north of Haiti, for example, many authorities have simply abdicated to American forces, and in Port-au-Prince even routine police work is now sometimes referred to the Americans. I would like you to comment on that.

U.S. PARTICIPATION IN U.N. FORCE

The second question is, you have said that in a few months you expect to hand over to the U.N. forces control of Haiti and that about half of those forces would be Americans. What do you anticipate the total needed would be so that we could get some idea of how many Americans are going to be in Haiti after the U.N. takes over?

And, finally, do you have any criteria for determining that Haiti has been stabilized sufficiently in order that our troops can be withdrawn, and if so, what are these criteria?

NO ENLARGEMENT OF U.S. MISSION

Mr. DEUTCH. Mrs. Meyers, let me answer these questions, and maybe Strobe will want to enlarge upon them.

The first is that the mission that has been established for our troops in Haiti has not changed one bit from when the planning was taking place. There has been no change in the scope of the mission, no change in the activities.

Mrs. MEYERS. It sounds as if we are taking over the jobs of local officials and local police.

Mr. DEUTCH. I don't believe that that is the case. Routine police functions are not being performed by U.S. troops. And I will just ask at the conclusion of my remarks for General Sheehan to confirm that fact and expand upon it, or contradict the fact if that is what it should be.

CRITERIA FOR TRANSITION TO UNMIH

Secondly, I believe Strobe Talbott said that it is our plan that the extent of this multinational force operation would be less than 6 months, at which time we would have the transition to the United Nations mission in Haiti, UNMIH. At that time we would expect to have fewer than one-half, both military and nonmilitary U.S. contract personnel involved, of the maximum of UNMIH, which would be 6,000 people.

The third question, ma'am was——

Mrs. MEYERS. Do you have any criteria established for when things are truly stabilized enough in Haiti for us to leave and turn the mission over to the U.N.?

Mr. DEUTCH. Let me give you a process rather than specific criteria that the decision would be the decision taken by both the U.S. commander and the Secretary General on the advice of the U.S. commander of the multinational force. So the U.S. commander would have the authority to advise the Secretary General on the specific state of security in the country before such a transition took place.

Now, if I——

Mr. TALBOTT. Could I just, before General Sheehan contradicts Secretary Deutch, introduce one additional criterion of a political nature?

The Haitian constitution electoral calendar called for parliamentary elections at the end of this year, or at the latest, at the very beginning of next year.

Mrs. MEYERS. Has the date been set for those parliamentary elections?

Mr. TALBOTT. No, I don't believe so. It will probably be in December, but it could slip into January. But President Aristide has committed himself—enthusiastically, I might say—several times to making sure that those elections take place.

To come to your point, one thing that we would be looking at very carefully is those elections and that they take place in a free and fair manner. I think that that would be dramatic evidence that life is returning to normal and that democracy has been restored.

U.S. ACTIONS NOT INDICATIVE OF MISSION CREEP

General SHEEHAN. Congresswoman, in response to that, I think what they are referring to is the fact, after Saturday's events in Cap-Haitien when the Marines killed the police and the attaches that were in the police building, right after that, the citizens of Cap-Haitien took over another police station and disarmed them and turned in some 700 weapons.

In order to have an argument, you have to have two sides. And right now, the police are not in Cap-Haitien; they have disappeared—those that are still left. So the Marines that are up there and the Army forces that are up there are doing normal patrolling, patrolling that they would have done had both sides been there.

General Shelton has gone to Cedras and told him to redeploy additional forces up to Cap-Haitien that essentially can operate there. We are going to take some of the police that have been trained in Gitmo and move them up there to create a vetted FADH because that is de facto, what we have done.

The citizens of Haiti have vetted their own police department up in that area, and those that don't particularly want to perform properly have left. So we don't see that as mission creep, but rather a reality on the ground that the citizens have in fact disarmed their own police and are in the process of putting a police force in place that is going to work.

Mrs. MEYERS. And it does mean that any further Haitian-on-Haitian violence that takes place there, we will be in the middle of it, unless there are some others deployed there?

General SHEEHAN. We don't expect that level of violence to take place. The weapons are being turned in. And second, the police force coming out of Guantanamo Bay, Cuba are volunteers to go back, and they don't have the same bias toward violence that the previous force had.

COST OF HAITI OPERATION

Mrs. MEYERS. And, finally, Mr. Chairman, do we have any estimate of the total cost of the military operation, including the U.S. forces that will be there as part of the U.N.?

84-415 O - 94 - 2

Mr. DEUTCH. Mrs. Meyers, let me just say that there are estimates of the costs. They are highly uncertain. Let me give them to you roughly this way.

In fiscal 1994, that is, which is about to end here at the end of the month, roughly $50 million. During the coming fiscal year, estimates are varied but in the range of $400 to $500 million.

I would like to emphasize to you how uncertain these estimates are, because we don't know the scope fully or the length fully of this operation. I will, if you permit me, provide you the best estimates that we have for the record, but I want to stress that, in my judgment, it is very hard to make a full accounting today of the military expenditures.

There are, of course, in addition to that $200 million or so of assistance, economic assistance during fiscal 1995, and I would like to provide that for the record if that is satisfactory, ma'am.

Chairman HAMILTON. Would the gentlelady yield?

Your figure of $400 to $500 million is the Defense Department expense for 1995, is that correct?

Mr. DEUTCH. Mr. Chairman, that is right. And I want to allow myself, in addition to certainty, accuracy by giving you something for the record.

Chairman HAMILTON. Who can give us a total figure?

Mr. DEUTCH. I think I would like to do that for the record, sir. We will do it by fiscal year and add up both economic and military assistance and give you the best estimates.

Chairman HAMILTON. Do you have a figure in your mind now?

Mr. DEUTCH. My figure for the total would be under $1 billion, about, but I would like to get you this tabulated for the record, sir.

Chairman HAMILTON. We want an "all spigots estimate."

Mr. DEUTCH. An "all spigots" estimate, but it is highly varied.[1]

Chairman HAMILTON. Mr. Faleomavaega.

OAS ROLE IN HAITI

Mr. FALEOMAVAEGA. Thank you, Mr. Chairman.

Secretary Talbott, I would like to commend the President for making every effort to avert the invasion by inviting our former President Carter and General Powell and Senator Nunn to provide some form of a negotiation process to avert this invasion, and I commend the administration for that.

I have just come to realize that you mentioned earlier something about the OAS assisting with this process in resolving the serious problems that we face now in Haiti, and I was wondering if you could elaborate a little further exactly what the OAS has been doing. I have come to believe that Haiti is not even a member of the "Latin American country club," so to speak, and I was curious about that.

PROSPECTS FOR PROLONGED U.S. MILITARY PRESENCE

There are a couple of other questions. Seven million people live in Haiti; approximately 90 percent are in sheer poverty, and I was wondering if—in most realistic terms, if we could ever build a true

[1] The information appears in appendix 2.

democracy in that island country where they have never seriously given that kind of political maturity in providing for that.

My understanding is that, come October 15, President Aristide takes over the administration of Haiti. Suppose Mr. Aristide just is unable to provide law and order—possibly, further assassinations of some of the country's top leaders—and just cannot stabilize the political situation in Haiti, unless we continue to have a major presence of U.S. military forces there? What then is the President's option?

The question of the 60-day period, am I to understand that 18 days are now in the running as part of that 60-day grace period that the President has authorized to commit this form of policy in terms of our military presence there in Haiti?

And the Congress is going to adjourn next week, hopefully, and I am just curious what the President intends to do after that 60-day period, if the administration has clearly thought out options, or proposals to the Congress as to what to do afterwards.

ROLE OF OAS

Mr. TALBOTT. First, with regard to the OAS, let me be absolutely clear on one point. As a body, the Organization of American States has not explicitly endorsed this particular operation. However, over the past couple of years, the OAS has repeatedly taken steps, held meetings, passed resolutions, issued reports, which were both individually and cumulatively extremely helpful and supportive of our goal, which is the departure from power of the military junta and the restoration of President Aristide.

By the way, Haiti is very much a member of the Organization of American States. President Aristide's Ambassador to Washington, and several of his ministers and representatives have been taking part in meetings of the OAS in recent months.

OPTIMISM ON TRANSITION TO DEMOCRACY

With regard to the "maturity," to use your word, of Haitian democracy, we all recognize that Haitian democracy is in its infancy. It was born, one might say, in December of 1990, making it only 4 years old. But it is one of the premises of our policy, as Secretary Christopher has put it on several occasions, that it is precisely nascent or newborn democracies that need as much help as possible from the international community.

Our hope, encouraged and buttressed, I might say, by the experience of the past week or so, is that the transition back to the restored democracy in Haiti will be relatively smooth and peaceful. There are institutions in Haiti. There is a parliament in Haiti; it will be back in session, we believe, as early as tomorrow. I think that my colleagues, in particular, have already addressed how we are prepared to deal with the contingency of political violence.

But President Aristide and his colleagues have done everything they could; and I come back to the point I made earlier about the message of reconciliation and urging his followers not to seek vengeance that he has been putting out in recent days. President Aristide, I think, has increased the chances of a smooth and peaceful restoration, not just of democracy but of a broad-based democracy.

WAR POWERS CLOCK

Mr. FALEOMAVAEGA. On the question of a 60-day period, is it running now?

Mr. TALBOTT. I am not sure which 60-day period you are referring to.

Mr. FALEOMAVAEGA. The 60-day war powers of the President.

Mr. DEUTCH. We will have to get back to you, sir. Under the War Powers Resolution?

Mr. FALEOMAVAEGA. Yes.

Mr. TALBOTT. We, of course, filed a War Powers Report under—as required by the law.

Mr. FALEOMAVAEGA. My question to you gentlemen, if it is to your understanding that since our presence in Haiti now has been 18 days, is that part of the 60-day period? Is it running?

Mr. TALBOTT. I—of course, Secretary Deutch had a superb answer, which is that we will get back to you on that.

OAS POLICY ON INTERVENTION

Mr. FALEOMAVAEGA. One more question. I am glad that you have clarified the situation with the OAS. There is one principal element of the OAS, that we are a member of, and that is that one member state is not to invade another member state; and are we an exception to the rule, Mr. Secretary? Why are we doing this to Haiti?

Mr. TALBOTT. The word "invasion," which has been bandied around a lot, over the last months in particular, is really not the right word here. After all, we—by which I mean a multinational force made up of now 29 nations, including the United States—have intervened there at the request of and on behalf of the legitimately elected government, and I think it is clear from the reception that our forces have received in the streets of Port-au-Prince and Cap-Haitien and elsewhere, very much at the behest of and to the welcome of the Haitian people.

The Organization of American States is, of course, as the United States is, against invasion as traditionally or classically understood. But the OAS is very much on record as supporting the principle that the hemisphere as a whole must join forces to support democracy. And that is what happened here.

Mr. FALEOMAVAEGA. I am concerned about that. It is always easier to lend financial support, but I don't think that we could equate that with when our soldiers bleed and die in the field of battle.

I don't think that even the member states of OAS who financially support us in this effort—it is ironic that we don't see any presence of other military forces from the member states of OAS supporting us in this effort, other than pieces of paper and saying, yes, we do in principle, but never really put your money where the mouth is.

Mr. TALBOTT. If I could add a word or two to, I hope, reassure you on that point.

When Secretary Perry and General Shalikashvili were down in Port-au-Prince over the weekend, they met with, among others, representatives of some of the nations that will, indeed, be deployed to Haiti in the very near future. Members of the multinational force are in Puerto Rico right now in training, along with our own people. And the first group of MNF forces will be in Haiti in coming days before the end of this month.

Chairman HAMILTON. Mr. Rohrabacher.

CONTROVERSY SURROUNDING ARISTIDE

Mr. ROHRABACHER. Thank you, Mr. Chairman.

And Mr. Talbott, I know there is a tendency for people to ask a dozen questions, but at times, believe it or not, when you ask administration officials a question, they will try to use up all the time, instead of giving a simple answer, just so you won't get a second question in.

I would like to ask a simple question. My colleague asked whether or not you knew if President Aristide had ever supported necklacing. To your knowledge, has President Aristide ever supported the practice of necklacing?

Mr. TALBOTT. There is no yes or no answer to that, Congressman.

Mr. ROHRABACHER. I think that is good enough.

Mr. TALBOTT. I have read statements that have been attributed to President Aristide. And I have also, as of course has the administration as a whole, studied President Aristide's record while he was in power; and I think my earlier statements——

Mr. ROHRABACHER. Would you rule it out that this man has advocated the burning to death of his opponents?

Mr. TALBOTT. What is important is what President Aristide stood for when he was elected the President of Haiti.

Mr. ROHRABACHER. I take that as a no. Anybody in this room knows that we are dealing with a man who, while in power, threatened to burn to death his opponents. Why are we sending U.S. Marines to Haiti to put this man back in power? Is that the great cause of democracy that you are talking about?

Mr. TALBOTT. Congressman, the cause of democracy is embodied in institutions of the kind that will be meeting in Port-au-Prince tomorrow.

Let me just say that I came relatively recently to this issue. I had followed a lot of the debate and controversy about President Aristide. I have had a chance in my present capacity to meet with him and to work with him, along with other members of the administration. And I would like to say here that it is an understatement to say that he does not live up to the stereotypes that we all are familiar with.

I think that President Aristide has in many ways gotten a bum rap over the last couple of years. And I think that he has demonstrated by the way that he has handled this transitional period his commitment to reconciliation.

Mr. ROHRABACHER. Let's hope that you are correct because American lives are on the line, and I would hate to think that we are putting not only the lives of our people on the line, but also our national treasure to reinstall this man. We are talking about hundreds of millions, if not billions of dollars, for a man who, while in power earlier, threatened to burn to death his opponents.

Mr. Talbott, I don't believe that this administration has defined for the American people this mission. I don't believe that the Haitian occupation is justified in terms of a national interest of the

United States. People keep asking why we are in Haiti. Yet, we haven't received an answer to our question.

Is this the reason why you didn't bother coming to Congress before the occupation to seek our advice and our consent?

RATIONALE FOR INTERVENTION

Mr. TALBOTT. A number of us, quite a number of us, have been coming to Congress repeatedly to consult with this body and, of course, with the Senate; and in the course of those consultations, we have repeated what we feel is the foreign policy and national security rationale for this policy.

Mr. ROHRABACHER. Do you believe that the President now has authority to militarily occupy any country in this hemisphere in which a democratically elected official is ousted, without consenting Congress?

Mr. TALBOTT. The President, of course, would make no such claim with regard to this policy or in general.

Mr. ROHRABACHER. So Haiti is just an aberration?

Mr. TALBOTT. It is by no means an aberration. It is an episode in which the United States had an opportunity, in coalition with others from this hemisphere and elsewhere, to support what has been an immensely positive trend in the Western Hemisphere over the last 15 or 20 years, and that is the trend of democratization.

Another element of it, which we have discussed in the course of this hearing, is that the opposite of democratization, that is, a terror-based dictatorship, was producing a humanitarian and human rights catastrophe, one result of which was a refugee outflow that impinged on our national security.

LACK OF CONGRESSIONAL CONSULTATION

Mr. ROHRABACHER. I would just like to state for the record, that I worked in the White House for 7 years. I know that the President has to make tough decisions, and I know that sometimes he doesn't have time to go to Congress. I understand that.

This was not one of those situations! If it was, I would be more understanding and the rest of your colleagues on the other side of the aisle would be understanding as well.

I feel, and many other members of this body feel, that it is an insult to our democratic institutions for the President of the United States to be spending so much time seeking permission from the United Nations about a military mission of American troops and then ignoring the U.S. Congress.

You are here seeking our cooperation now. You are asking us not to set a time deadline because it might jeopardize your mission. I would suggest that the President of the United States should have had a cooperative mood and a cooperative method with Congress before he sent in our U.S. military, and he might be getting more cooperation right now had he done so.

Thank you very much.

Chairman HAMILTON. Mr. Oberstar.

ADEQUACY OF CONSULTATION

Mr. OBERSTAR. Thank you, Mr. Chairman.

Thank you, Secretary Talbott, for being with us today, as you have on many occasions; and I think shortly after taking your new position, you were up here before this committee talking with us about Haiti.

I differ with my colleague from California. There have been numerous consultations in this committee room, informal and in formal session, numerous opportunities. I think there were more than 70 or 80 such opportunities for discussion on Haiti over a long period of time. And this administration has been totally open. And the Bush administration was very open with its policy on Haiti. And I participated in numerous discussions with that leadership, as well, I would say to my colleague from California.

Let's not have a double standard. You know, if this were a different administration, we would be hearing a totally different song from the other side of the aisle, frankly; and I don't care what kind of justification you come up with, there are some people who will never be satisfied. They just want to embarrass the President. Let's lay it out as it is.

SUCCESS OF U.S. POLICY

The question is—the test is really the success of the policy. And our forces went in in a peaceful intervention. They were greeted with shouts of joy by the Haitian people. It was something I said would happen, that that would be the response from the people of Haiti. They looked to the United States as their source of support, their friend, their salvation. And you have seen the joy on the faces of the people in Haiti.

I was there. I was a part of the observer team that President Bush sent to observe the elections in Haiti. I thought the Bush administration policy was right on every step of the way and brought that democracy about. I was a part of helping it to happen.

The general, the commanding general of the armed forces at the time was General Gerard Abraham, who was a second lieutenant in one of my English courses when I taught English in Haiti. I taught English and not civics, I want to emphasize.

But I did talk at length with General Abraham on many occasions both by phone and in person. And he made the election come about. He assured that there was tranquility at the polls, that there was no shooting and not a repeat of the sabotage of the election of November of 1987. And we did have a peaceful and a responsible, honest election.

And as I talked to the people as they were leaving the voting places and asked them, "Pouqui sa ou te vote?" Why did you vote? What did you vote for?

"Na vote libete-a." We voted for freedom.

They didn't say, we voted for a better economic life. They didn't say, we voted to end the World Bank debt. They didn't say, we voted for jobs. They voted for freedom from the Ton-tons Macoutes and from the Duvalierism, and that freedom was snatched from them in the coup of September 1991.

And we have restored that freedom to them, or an opportunity for that freedom, and I don't want to let it slip from our grasp.

This has been an effort of several years, over three administrations, to bring this result about. And I say, let's stand and support this policy. The Haitian people will be in our debt for a long time. They will have an opportunity—they can govern themselves. We just removed the yoke of the army of oppression from their back.

DISARMAMENT PROGRAM

And I have other suggestions about getting into the countryside and taking the guns. I don't think that the policy of buying the guns is going to be very effective. I think you need to seize the stocks of the Ton-tons Macoutes—the army knows where they are and how to get them—and take them out of their hands so that in the aftermath of the departure that we don't, "Se lave mains, essie pa te," the Haitian proverb that says: Don't wash your hands and then dry them off in the dirt.

And if we don't get those guns out of the hands of the thugs, the Macoutes who have used them, we will be, "Se lave mains, essie pa te".

Thank you, Mr. Chairman.

Chairman HAMILTON. Mr. Oberstar is the committee linguist, as you may know.

Mr. Manzullo.

ARISTIDE'S RECORD

Mr. MANZULLO. Thank you, Mr. Chairman. I think Mr. Oberstar's statement today is the exact reason why Congress should be consulted, to have the input of people of his wisdom in addition to the wisdom of Mr. Talbott.

You are on record today as saying that Aristide has gotten a bum rap. Let me give you three reasons why that is a disservice to the U.S. people for you to say that.

He was removed from the church celestial order because of incitement to hatred and violence.

Number two, when he assumed power, he named supreme court justices, including the chief justice, without seeking the approval of the democratically elected Senate. He also replaced democratically elected mayors in key Haitian cities all on his own.

And the third reason is this quote from his autobiography, page 126: I welcome those ideas that rest on the values of beauty, dignity, respect and love. Che Guevara—a bourgeoisie, a doctor, internationalist—certainly incorporated some of those values, as did Allende. They were severe men. They made mistakes, just as I will do. Why should I deny it? I feel more affection and sympathy for them than I do for many others.

Sending American soldiers into harm's way to instill a man who was a lover of Che Guevara, and you say he has gotten a bum rap? These are his own words from his own autobiography. Mr. Talbott, we are engaged in voodoo diplomacy. The United States has no interest in Haiti.

QUESTIONING U.S. POLICY GOALS

And I have been ticking off the things that have been stated in your own words. We are going to build a civilian and democratic police force. With what tools? We have just been told that those

Haitians supposedly in exile in Guantanamo Bay, will be the police force.

We have been told that we are there for the purpose of long-term U.S. credibility. Nobody in the Congress believes you. The American people don't believe you. We have been told by Mr. Deutch our military mission is, "to establish a secure environment in Haiti and assist a transition to a stable government,".

And then we were told that the U.S. commander will advise the Secretary General of the U.N. Who determines when we pull out? The United States or the United Nations?

And then we were told by General Sheehan, who has a very difficult job, that the police force was to come from the exiles at Guantanamo Bay. And I would presume that he is saying that because those are the orders that he has. But what is most amazing to me is that when the Members of Congress were briefed by General Powell, Senator Nunn and Mr. Christopher, who should have been here also today, about 140 members had questions. Who will be retraining the police force? And the answer came, well, the current police force will be retraining themselves.

Now, when you are putting back in power somebody who loves Che Guevara and somebody who has a disdain for peace as we know it in this country, and he will ultimately be in charge of the police, how could we say with any certainty that when we withdraw from Haiti, the situation at that point will improve?

DEFENSE OF ARISTIDE

Mr. TALBOTT. Mr. Chairman, I think that Secretary Deutch may want to say a word or two more just to clarify this all-important issue of how we propose working with the international community and the Government of Haiti to establish an interim police force. I think for very understandable reasons some clarification is required there.

Let me just say the following with respect to President Aristide. I understand, of course, the thrust of those points you have chosen to highlight from his biography. I would suggest, respectfully, that President Aristide's views on Che Guevara are not the most germane fact here. The most germane fact is that in December of 1990, 90 percent of the Haitian people went to the polls and voted in a free and fair election and 67.5 percent of those voters voted for President Aristide.

Mr. MANZULLO. Based upon that, you say that this man believes in the peaceful democratic process as we do. Hitler was elected peacefully.

Mr. TALBOTT. President Aristide, even in recent days, I think, has reestablished—and I stress reestablished, in deed as well as in word, his commitment to a process.

Mr. MANZULLO. He is telling you that because that is what you want to hear. He wrote in his autobiography that he has an infatuation with Che Guevara. Now he is going to be in charge of this police force? That doesn't make sense.

REBUILDING THE HAITIAN POLICE FORCE

Mr. TALBOTT. Maybe this would be an appropriate point to clarify a little bit about the police force. We have probably spent as much time within the government on the issue of police as any other single dimension of this very complicated operation over the last few months. And the reason, I think, is implicit in the discussion we are having here today.

Part of the mission is to establish the conditions of essential civic order; that is a responsibility that must rest on Haitian soldiers. The U.S. military is not going to be in the position in an open-ended way of being the cop on the beat in Haiti. So we have spent a great deal of time working on this.

It is our plan, which we are quite optimistic we are going to be able to carry out, that we, working with the Government of Haiti, will be able to identify somewhere between 1,500 and 2,000 personnel from the current armed forces of Haiti. These are people who have been just doing a job—they do not have a record of human rights violations or anything like that—and will be available to serve as an interim police force that can be augmented by other sources.

The Haitian Government is now in Guantanamo, as General Sheehan said, working with 1,200 to 1,500 of the refugees there who are police trainees, and it will be a key function of the United Nations mission when it comes in after the conclusion of the multinational force to complete the process of professionalizing the police force.

But perhaps Secretary Deutch could be given a chance to add a few words.

Mr. OBERSTAR [presiding]. Briefly. Other members are waiting.

U.S. RETAINS AUTHORITY OVER TROOPS

Mr. DEUTCH. Congressman, I regret that I made my point and you misunderstood it, exactly the reverse. That is that the United States has full authority over all of its troops. It makes the decision when they are coming out, at what pace and when; and the United Nations Secretary General cannot make a decision without the advice of the United States commander.

So it is exactly the opposite of the way you interpreted it. I regret that fact.

We call the shots on when our troops come out, and the transition cannot be made without our participation by the Secretary General.

Mr. OBERSTAR. The gentleman's time has expired.

Mr. Menendez.

SOURCE OF FUNDING FOR HAITI OPERATION

Mr. MENENDEZ. Thank you.

Secretary Talbott, I have about four questions. Most of them could be answered by you, but I would be happy to hear your colleagues add if they wish.

One is, I heard Secretary Deutch say, in response to the questions that I intended to ask as well about the amounts of monies to be spent, saying that for 1994 it is $50 million, an estimate for the upcoming year is $400 to $500 million. And you said that it is uncertain and it is hard to make accountings, but you are going to try; this is your best estimate. I assume that means that it could be greater or could it be less.

Mr. DEUTCH. Both, sir.

Mr. MENENDEZ. It could go either way. Added to $200 to $300 million in AID assistance that we are contemplating, are we not heading toward the billion dollar mark in this whole proposal?

And, secondly, where are we taking—especially when I think of AID, where are we taking those monies from? For those of us on this committee who have been arguing that certain parts of the world automatically get raided in that context, I would like to know where it is that that money is coming from.

AMNESTY FOR COUP LEADERS CRITICIZED

In the context of human rights and democracy that Secretary Christopher has said were the pillars of foreign diplomacy of this administration, I wonder out loud, what is it when we, in fact, have the President of the United States saying that General Cedras and Francois and company are among the worst human rights abusers, not in the world, but certainly in the hemisphere? Some of us shudder when we think of others who are even worse human rights abusers, but the bottom line is that they are among the worst human rights abusers, and yet they walk away with an agreement that says they can walk away basically with amnesty, without an obligation to leave the country—maybe an expectation, but without an obligation to leave the country—and that whatever resources they may have may very well end up being their own when this is all over.

What does that say to those we are trying to fight on respect for human rights and democracy in other parts of the world? Does it say that if you hang out there long enough we will make a deal with you and you can walk away with the proceeds of what you raped a country with and with your actions gone untouched?

POLICY ON U.S. DEPARTURE

Thirdly, it is maybe a minor question in the context of this, but did I not hear the President give his national address. Is the concern over refugees now part of what we would consider the national security interests?

And lastly, what are the set of circumstances in which we will leave Haiti? And I have heard you talk about the U.N. mission, and I have heard you say that, in fact, we will make a certification to the U.N. that it is secure and safe and whatnot. But I would like to hear what are the standards that you will use to determine that your certification to the United Nations is appropriate, and when do you expect the timeframe for that to be? And I assume that you can give us some sense of a timeframe if you can state what you think is going to be your costs. Your cost is obviously driven by your manpower and the period of time in which you, in fact, expect to be there. So I would assume you can give us some sense of time, even if you don't want to have a date certain hanging over your head.

ECONOMIC ASSISTANCE

Mr. TALBOTT. Thank you, Congressman. On the first question with regard to economic assistance, as Secretary Deutch has promised you, we will, of course, be coming back to you with a very precise and thorough projection of costs, including in that area.[2]

President Clinton, in his speech to the United Nations yesterday, made clear that we feel that it is very important if this mission is going to succeed that there be an economic assistance component to it as well.

I would stress several things. First of all, this is not something that the United States will be doing alone. Our Agency for International Development has been working with other nations and with the international financial institutions, the InterAmerican Development Bank, the World Bank in particular, in order to put together a package that will be appropriate. There is already $100 million in the fiscal year 1995 budget for use in Haiti.

We feel that we will need another $100 million, which, of course, goes to the second part of your question. Obviously, we are in an era of limited resources, and we will be consulting very closely with the Congress on identifying sources for those funds.

RATIONALE FOR AGREEMENT WITH COUP LEADERS

With regard to how history, as well as our administration, judges General Cedras, General Biamby and Colonel Francois, I would simply say on that score that President Clinton's depiction of them, which you have referred to, was fully justified, remains fully justified, and stands as far as we are concerned.

Mr. MENENDEZ. Mr. Secretary, I don't mean history, I mean, what is the message that we send to others similarly situated?

Mr. TALBOTT. As a result of the agreement reached in Port-au-Prince a week ago Sunday, two things were achieved. A date certain for the departure from power of Cedras, Biamby and Francois, and an arrangement—an arrangement with the military regime there and the de facto government that permitted the peaceful deployment of American forces, thus saving American and Haitian lives. We think it was a good agreement, for that reason, and I stress both halves of that.

Now, what will the fate of General Cedras and the other two be after the restoration of the democratic government? We have said repeatedly that we believe that they should not only leave power, but that they should leave Haiti.

That was not provided for in the Port-au-Prince agreement, but that issue will be resolved in the future in which reality will have changed considerably in Haiti. Whether they will be beneficiaries of the amnesty that will be discussed by the Haitian Parliament when it reconvenes tomorrow is up to the Haitian Parliament.

Mr. OBERSTAR. Mr. Gilman.

Mr. GILMAN. Thank you, Mr. Chairman. I too want to welcome our panelists for joining us and I do have just a few questions.

CONSIDERATIONS GUIDING U.S. POLICY

Mr. MENENDEZ. Mr. Gilman, would you yield for one moment?

Mr. Chairman, I would hope that—while my time to ask questions had expired, I had two outstanding questions that didn't get answered—that they could be answered verbally or in writing.

---

[2] See appendix 2.

Mr. OBERSTAR. The chair asks the witnesses to respond to the remaining questions in writing.

Mr. TALBOTT. I was aware of that, Mr. Menendez, and I will try to be responsive on the third of the four questions that you asked.

Mr. DEUTCH. I would also like to respond to the fourth.

Mr. TALBOTT. Yes, the issue of refugees is a consideration and an important consideration in this policy. The policy——

Mr. OBERSTAR. Mr. Talbott, I know you have a time limitation here, and the length of your responses is going to determine how long you are going to stay here.

Mr. TALBOTT. I understand that, but I do feel that the Congressman deserves an answer on that, as have others.

Mr. OBERSTAR. I understand that. We have a lot of members that have——

Mr. TALBOTT. The other components were democracy, human rights; and taken together, they made up the national rationale for this policy.

CRITIQUE OF U.S. POLICY

Mr. GILMAN. We support the ideals of constitutional democracy and recognize the need for respect for human rights in Haiti. President Aristide is certainly a powerful symbol for many of us with regard to democracy and social justice. But many of us remain unconvinced that only men with military force could achieve those worthy objectives; and by intervening in Haiti our Nation has taken sides in a country with a long history of bloody civil unrest and no tradition of political conciliation.

Our policymakers have ignored the costly and bitter lesson of our occupation of Haiti that ended some 60 years ago, and regrettably, they seem to be ignoring the lessons that we should have learned in Somalia. By improvising rules of engagement and committing ourselves to an overambitious mission, it seems that we are repeating the lessons that we didn't learn in Somalia.

I will conclude with just this note. If the President wants to rewrite the rules for engaging American military forces, even when no vital U.S. interests are at stake, those should be debated in the Congress, fully. Secondly, we have seen no reliable assessment of what the intervention and subsequent reconstruction and development of Haiti will cost the American taxpayer.

I am pleased that Secretary Deutch will forward information on costs to us—I asked at the last briefing that we had last week, and we were assured by Secretary Perry that that information would be provided to us.

Third, our Nation is doing and paying more than its fair share to restore order in a country that has never known it. Our President's key objectives, which he laid out for the American people—restoring President Aristide, removing the military junta, and addressing human rights—can be addressed in a matter of a few weeks. Beyond that, we drift into nation-building and prolonged occupation, which will galvanize Haitian nationalism and could exact a terrible price.

Along with that, I would like to ask our panel this: When will the U.N. peacekeeping mission be prepared to take over for the multinational force, and just how extensive is that mission? As far

84-415 O - 94 - 3

as I can see, there are only about a handful of nations, most of them in the CARICOM, who have offered some help, and just one or two of the Latin American countries. I think Bolivia, Argentina and maybe one or two in Central America.

I think the whole offer of help is 2,400 in personnel. And the President talked about a 6,000 peacekeeping force, and so did our briefers last week. Where is that help going to come from? How many peacekeepers are we going to need and how many of them are going to be U.S. troops?

COMPOSITION OF MULTINATIONAL FORCE

Mr. TALBOTT. Taking the last point first, Congressman, in the multinational force phase, which will involve about a 2,500 force, it is actually quite a wide geographical reach.

Mr. GILMAN. That is 2,500 without United States being counted?

Mr. TALBOTT. That is correct, 2,500. In addition to Latin American countries and Caribbean countries, there are also European countries involved—Belgium, Holland, at least one African country, Benin, Poland.

Mr. GILMAN. I am talking about the Latin American troops. I know we have got some offers from other countries, but how many from——

Mr. TALBOTT. These are not just offers, incidentally; these are commitments. These are troops who in many cases are already in Puerto Rico.

Mr. GILMAN. 2,500 is the number?

Mr. TALBOTT. Twenty-eight nations and 2,500 personnel.

Mr. GILMAN. And the rest of them will be United States, and we are still talking about 6,000 peacekeepers?

TIMETABLE FOR TRANSITION TO U.N. FORCE

Mr. TALBOTT. The second phase—this is a U.S.-dominant operation at the beginning. There is no question that it has always been conceived that way. But quickly, we believe that we can draw down the American component and hand this over to the United Nations peacekeeping operation, no more than half of which will be Americans.

Mr. GILMAN. When do you anticipate that we could do that?

Mr. TALBOTT. We would hope that would be in a matter of months, in the beginning of next year.

Mr. GILMAN. By January, we would be in a position to turn it all over to the peacekeepers?

Mr. TALBOTT. That would certainly be a hope, but in the context of earlier discussion, I would just emphasize on behalf of the three of us and the administration once again that there is all the difference in the world between a plan which we are quite optimistic about being able to keep and a mandated date certain for withdrawal.

Mr. GILMAN. When do you think that the bulk of our troops that have gone in in the last week or two will be coming out?

Mr. DEUTCH. Mr. Gilman, in brief, the plan calls for, within 6 months, to have U.S. forces drawn down considerably to the level of roughly 3,000 or so, which would be the share that we would expect at maximum would be present by the United States in the United Nations mission in Haiti.

Mr. GILMAN. We think that we could get them out by January?

Mr. DEUTCH. Six months. The plan calls for 6 months from the date of the beginning of the operation in September, so I think that brings us to March. Now, it would be—we are all hoping to do it earlier, but 6 months has been the planning date that we have continually——

Mr. GILMAN. Have you started to remove some of our troops now?

Mr. DEUTCH. We will begin to remove some of our troops as early as next week.

Mr. GILMAN. Who is going to command the U.N. peacekeeping mission?

Mr. DEUTCH. Excellent question, Mr. Gilman. We hope, and trust, that we can have an American commander. We are certainly hoping for that.

Mr. GILMAN. We are hoping, but do we know? Is that some problem?

Mr. DEUTCH. I don't think that that has been completely agreed upon. But it is certainly our expectation that it will be a U.S. commander.

PEACEKEEPING COSTS

Mr. GILMAN. When you give us the costs of our mission to date, would you also give us a projected cost of our peacekeeping.

Mr. DEUTCH. Everywhere in the world, sir?

Mr. GILMAN. No, I am referring now—I thought the subject of this was Haiti.

Mr. DEUTCH. I am sorry, sir. I thought you were asking for the peacekeeping operations everywhere.

Mr. GILMAN. I am talking about the peacekeeping costs in Haiti.

Mr. DEUTCH. Of course, sir.

Mr. GILMAN. When we can anticipate that? Last week Secretary Perry said that we could anticipate that in a few days.

Mr. DEUTCH. Tomorrow, sir.

Mr. GILMAN. Mr. Chairman, if we could make that a part of the record.

Chairman HAMILTON [presiding]. Without objection.[3]

Ms. McKinney.

DEPARTURE OF COUP LEADERS

Ms. MCKINNEY. Thank you, Mr. Chairman. I would just like to commend our three panelists for being up here so long and facing sometimes unnecessarily hostile questions. I would also like to commend you for your thoroughness—and you definitely are prepared—and your responsiveness.

I have a question about the departure of Cedras, Francois and Biamby. I am wondering what kind of assurance we have that on October 15 they will indeed step down from power.

Two, what kind of assurance do we have that they will leave the island; and three, inasmuch as we might be marking up a resolution that contains a date certain for our departure, how does that

---

[3] The information appears in appendix 2.

date certain impact the behavior—our expected behavior as far as Cedras, Francois and Biamby are concerned?

Mr. TALBOTT. We are, I think I can say, totally confident that General Cedras, Biamby and Francois will step down, which is to say, give up all political power on October 15 under the terms of the agreement to which they are committed. And our reason for that is the American military presence and the multinational force in Haiti.

And I might say—and General Sheehan may want to comment on this, because his colleagues are working directly with General Cedras in order to effect the transition of power there. But it is my understanding that everything we have seen suggests that that is, indeed, their intention; and we certainly have the wherewithal to make it happen in any event.

On the second question of their leaving Haiti—and I realize I am now going back over ground covered earlier. It is not provided for in the Port-au-Prince agreement signed a week ago Sunday; nonetheless, it remains our view that they should leave. And we think there is a good chance that they will when they are confronted with the new political and other realities in Haiti.

On the effect of a legislative date certain for withdrawal with regard to those three, I would simply say that the point I made in general applies in the specific case, that a congressionally mandated date certain for withdrawal, I am concerned, might embolden those who do not want to see the restoration of democracy there.

Ms. MCKINNEY. Thank you, Mr. Chairman.

Chairman HAMILTON. Mr. Roth.

AMERICAN PUBLIC OPINION ON HAITI INTERVENTION

Mr. ROTH. Thank you, Mr. Chairman. The more I see of this Haiti, reminds me of when I was a young man there was a movie that was quite popular, The Mouse that Roared. A small country declared a war on the United States to get foreign aid, and it seems to be playing out somewhat here.

Last year Secretary Christopher was before our committee, and he said in committing U.S. forces, there were four criteria that this administration has adopted. One was that it had a clear goal; two, support of the American people; three, a reasonable chance for success; and four, a plan to get out.

Would you please tell me how these criteria have been met in Haiti?

Mr. TALBOTT. We have a clear goal. It is the restoration of the legitimate, democratically elected government of that country. We are quite confident about having a reasonable chance of success; I would say even better than that. We did not go in without a clear notion, both of how we will get out and when we will get out. There has been a lot of discussion about that here.

On the question of support of the American people, there is no question whatsoever, Congressman, that this is a highly controversial, much-debated and indeed much-opposed policy. On that score, I would only echo what President Clinton has said on a couple of occasions; and that is, to their credit, the American people are almost always reluctant to see force used. That has been the case in virtually every exertion of American force that we have seen, and

I think it speaks well both for the prudence and the peace-loving nature of the American people.

It is the administration's hope that as they see this drama unfold in coming days and weeks, they will feel what those of us in the administration feel, and I hope many outside of the administration feel as well, and that is not only pride in what our young men and women in the armed services are doing there, but also will see a vindication of the political mission.

Mr. ROTH. Well, if I can respond, I would say, a chance for getting out, I think that is—from the answers we heard here today, it is nebulous at best. As far as reasonable chance for a success, there is a civil war going on in Haiti between these different factions and you are not going to reestablish peace by putting 15,000 Americans into Haiti to try to establish peace among 6 or 7 million people.

As far as support of the American people, well, if the American people are wise—and they are—this is their government; why don't we listen to them? Why did we go into Haiti? I don't think that has ever been answered.

As far as a clear goal for success, when is this election with Aristide going to take place? Because according to the President, we are going to stay there until this election is going to take place.

Mr. TALBOTT. December 1995, and his successor will be installed in February 1996.

COMPOSITION OF MULTINATIONAL FORCE

Mr. TALBOTT. The multinational force phase of this, which is the one that most Americans will be involved, will be finished long, long before that; and we have talked a little bit about the timeframe of that here. The United Nations mission which will come in after the multinational force would be mandated to remain until February 1996.

Mr. ROTH. Isn't this multinational force really a deception?

Let's be frank. Let's put all the cards on the table. You said 2,500 from 28 different countries. The Americans are going to do the heavy lifting. This multinational force is a deception on the American people to say that there are others than Americans involved. I have seen all of these multinational forces before. It amounts to 50 people from here, 25 doctors from some other country, 100 people from somewhere else, and Americans are doing all the heavy lifting.

Mr. TALBOTT. Let me just—and General Sheehan has a word or two to say on this, as well—the police function and the police monitoring function is absolutely critical to the overall success of this. Virtually all of the police monitors will be drawn from the multinational force.

General SHEEHAN. This is not a place where there is an assault combat requirement. This is a stability force operation. Colonel Graham and his Caribbean force is a professionally well trained force, as is the Bangladeshi battalion that is coming in. And the Israelis are as good as you can get in the police business, and so I would give them very high marks.

Mr. ROTH. Well, the Israelis right now are debating whether or not they are going to come; isn't that true?

General SHEEHAN. Yes, sir.

Mr. ROTH. So what I am saying is that you get a few people from 28 other countries and you say it is a multinational force. No, it is not; that is just window dressing. Americans are doing all the work. And I think that you have an obligation to tell the American people that, General.

General SHEEHAN. Sir, the forces that are coming in clearly intend to carry their load.

Mr. TALBOTT. I would just say, Congressman, that in all the consultations that we have had with your colleagues, we have taken pains to lay out exactly what the role would be of the international participants, as well as the American role; and what we are seeing unfold coincides with the plan.

U.S. RESPONSE TO POTENTIAL CEDRAS CANDIDACY

Mr. ROTH. I just have one more question. If Cedras runs for President—and he may well do that—and he wins, are we going to back him?

Mr. TALBOTT. The United States stands for democracy and that means free and fair elections and the result of free and fair elections.

Mr. ROTH. So the answer is yes. If he wins, we will back him?

Mr. TALBOTT. Rather than addressing it in a hypothetical, with a specific personality, I would just underscore the principle.

Mr. ROTH. But it is not a hypothetical; it is very straightforward.

Mr. TALBOTT. With respect, I would suggest that at this point it is quite hypothetical. But I believe I have been responsive to your question. The reason that we are in Haiti today is because the Haitian people had a chance to conduct a free and fair election, and they elected a government. That government was overthrown by a coup d'etat and that coup d'etat is about to be reversed and the democratically elected government is going to be given a chance to go back in.

Mr. ROTH. And if Cedras runs for President and he wins, then we are going too back him because we back any——

Mr. TALBOTT. We will continue to support the workings of democracy.

Chairman HAMILTON. The gentleman's time his expired. We are going to have to conclude the hearing. The bells have rung for a vote. We have two members remaining, Mr. Payne and Mr. Hastings. I will have to ask them to share the time and I regret that. Mr. Payne and then Mr. Hastings.

Mr. PAYNE. I yield to Mr. Hastings. And then I will take the last question.

DEFENSE OF U.S. POLICY TOWARD HAITI

Mr. HASTINGS. Thank you for yielding and thank you, Mr. Chairman.

I would like to briefly disabuse my colleague, Mr. Roth, of a couple of theories, one being the notion that there was and is a civil war in Haiti. At least it is not a shooting civil war because the military junta has been in control of all the circumstances.

Another is the notion that American soldiers in this particular effort under Phase One of U.N. Security Council Resolution 940 are doing the heavy lifting. I believe that all of the presenters would agree that that is the case. But I would remind you that there are 19 peacekeeping missions ongoing in the world today.

I happened to see one in Croatia where 27,000 ground personnel are involved and not a single American soldier is there. Of those 67,000, less than 2,000 of them are American soldiers.

We are about the business of being involved after the post-cold war era in something more than war-making; it is now peace-making. And I see no reason at all why if everyone else is turning to the United Nations we, as the remaining superpower of the world, shouldn't be the leaders in peacekeeping efforts.

As we speak, this Nation—and this is directed to my colleague, Mr. Rohrabacher, as he leaves—in calling—I was going to tell you whether you were here or not—the notion about Aristide; let me make it clear. I don't support necklacing, and I don't believe anybody does. But we are meeting with Yeltsin from the Russian Government and the Russian Government and the former Soviet Union committed atrocities that would dwarf the human rights violations of many other countries in the world.

We have MFN in China, and we know all the circumstances there. This is a different world. And the fact of the matter is that other people change. I have been a critic of these same persons who are here today and that is the upshot of all of my remarks, Mr. Talbott. We are there not only at the behest of the elected representatives, but we are at the behest of the United Nations; and fortuitously, because of the success of the Carter mission, we are also there because of the de facto government and their invitation pursuant to whatever that agreement was in Port-au-Prince.

I don't feel President Clinton has failed in foreign policy, and I keep hearing that garbage from my colleagues on the other side of the aisle. In Somalia, we saved 1 million lives. In Bosnia, as I indicated, no American ground forces are involved at all. North Korea was a volatile kettle of confusion a few days ago; now it has more stability to it. We are dealing with Russia, and in Africa we have done extraordinary things.

The policy that you all asked for is a correct policy, and I hesitate, because I am very supportive of the chairman of this committee—I don't think that we should have a date certain, and the reason is not tying the President's hands or whether the President came here and consulted—and I can concur with many of the remarks that have been made. The fact is, I don't want to tie those kids' hands, who are on the ground, and that is where the action is and I don't think that in many respects we should.

PUBLIC OPINION ON HAITI POLICY

Let me say finally, Mr. Chairman, I heard Mr. Torricelli talk about what overwhelming sentiment is in America today. And, Don, I apologize for taking the added time, but I sat here and fumed when I heard what overwhelming sentiment is.

Let me tell you where overwhelming sentiment came from. Overwhelming sentiment as regards Haiti came as questions put by pollsters to the effect of would you invade Haiti? The answer to that is no. If you asked if you knew that invading Haiti would stop Haitians from coming to America and would save American dollars and give democracy a chance to flourish and would cause taxpayers in other communities throughout the world not to have to suffer abuse of their systems, either socially, hospital-wise, or school-wise, would you favor intervention to stop that? The answer is yes, without hesitancy.

It is time for us to get on with this business.

One word of caution on the buy-back, Mr. Deutch. Make sure that the Dominican border is not a place where added arms can come through.

And I thank you all so very much, and I thank President Clinton, and President Carter and Colin Powell and Senator Nunn and all of the people that are involved; and I will stand toe to toe with anybody on the other side and tell them that I think that this administration deserves a round of applause and immense credit and commendation.

And I thank you, Mr. Chairman.

Chairman HAMILTON. Mr. Payne.

WORLD OPINION ON U.S. INTERVENTION

Mr. PAYNE. Thank you very much. Since there is very little time left, I would certainly associate myself with the remarks of my colleague from Florida. I would also like to indicate that being at the U.N. yesterday and talking to a number of the delegates from other countries, there was a tremendous amount of praise for the stand that the United States made and for its decision to act and to act in a very strong and forceful way.

And so I was very proud yesterday, on the floor of the U.N., in conversations with many people, to see the U.S.A. being talked about in more glowing terms about its resolve.

I think that what has been indicated earlier about regional areas being—I disagree with Mr. Torricelli talking about this is neocolonialism. The reasons that we were in Haiti before and in Latin and Central America is a lot different from the reasons that we are going back.

And I think the debate is whether Japan ought to take more of a role in the Pacific and whether Russia, under the U.N., should take more responsibility in the New Independent States, and I think that in Africa whether the stronger African nations, South Africa, should take a role in peacekeeping; and I think the only way to go is through the United Nations with the stronger powers being able to have governance. If we have a world without governance, without policing, then we have a chaotic place.

OPPOSITION TO TERMINATION DATE

And so I would also like to say that I think a date certain would be a tragedy. I think that it does not make sense. You cannot do a job like you are attempting to do with a date certain. You have a plan. Every plan needs to be modified every once in a while. But to tie the hands of the administration I think would be a big mistake. And I would hope that all of my patriotic friends on the other side of the aisle would remember that as we are talking about lives of U.S. military personnel being in harm's way and the threat, that when they make this a partisan issue this, is not partisan, those young people are there—Democrat, Republican or Independent, or whatever, they are there because it was a decision that they made. But I just hate to see continuing this partisanism in this policy.

Concluding, I would like to commend the President again for staying the course, and making an unpopular decision. But it took us 10 years after World War II because that was unpopular, too, as a matter of fact. The majority of the people opposed World War II when we declared war on Germany on December 8 after the bombing on December 7.

There has not been a popular war period. Even the War of 1812 was unpopular.

And so, let me just say that it is not new; if you poll the people, they would say let's not go to war. People just don't like war in this country. But I think sometimes we have to—we are not at war, but sometimes we have to intervene militarily. As has been indicated, I don't think the War Powers Resolution applies here because we didn't intervene militarily, we used troops to go in, not to wage any conflict.

So thank you very much, Mr. Chairman.

And with that, I will adjourn the meeting.

[Whereupon, at 4:45 p.m., the committee was adjourned.]

U.S. POLICY TOWARD, AND PRESENCE IN, HAITI—CONSIDERATION OF H.J. RES. 416

WEDNESDAY, SEPTEMBER 28, 1994

HOUSE OF REPRESENTATIVES,
COMMITTEE ON FOREIGN AFFAIRS,
Washington, DC.

The committee met, pursuant to call, at 10:40 a.m., in room 2172, Rayburn House Office Building, Hon. Lee H. Hamilton (chairman) presiding.

Chairman HAMILTON. The House Foreign Affairs Committee will come to order.

[Whereupon the committee proceeded to other business.]

Chairman HAMILTON. The next order of business is H.J. Res. 416. The joint resolution before the committee makes clear that the U.S. military mission in Haiti should be limited in time and scope, and that it should have clearly defined responsibilities.

First, the resolution authorizes the U.S. military presence in Haiti until March 1, 1995. Congress should share responsibility any time that U.S. troops are deployed abroad for possible combat purposes. Congress should be on record with respect to Haiti.

Most of our colleagues, I believe, want to set a deadline for our involvement in Haiti, and this resolution includes a deadline. A date earlier than March 1 for troop withdrawal is irresponsible from an institutional and operational standpoint. Our troops should not be abandoned in the field without congressional support. The authorization should not expire while Congress is out of session. Congress will not be sufficiently organized before March 1 to give this issue full consideration.

We should also provide the greatest chance for the success of the operation. We should do what we can to ensure an orderly transfer of the mission to a follow-on force. This resolution should provide sufficient time for transfer to the United Nations led force.

Second, the resolution makes clear that we are authorizing the deployment in Haiti for limited purposes. Those are to protect U.S. citizens, to stabilize the security situation so that orderly progress can be made in transferring the functions of government in Haiti to the democratically elected government, and to facilitate the provision of humanitarian assistance.

We are not authorizing nation building in the resolution, and we are not authorizing U.S. troops to build democracy. U.S. Armed Forces should not be running Haiti or rebuilding it. Military force cannot be expected to achieve anything beyond the purposes in the resolution. The job of rebuilding in Haiti should not fall on U.S.

Armed Forces. It is the responsibility of Haiti and the international community.

Third, this resolution guarantees that members of Congress will have the opportunity to vote again after March 1, 1995, if they do not approve the President's plan for a U.S. role in the United Nations led force. It provides expedited procedures for consideration of a joint resolution that would direct the President to withdraw all troops from Haiti.

Today is not the day to decide whether the United States should participate in the United Nations mission. The decision to participate in the United Nations mission should be made in the context of circumstances in Haiti at the time of the mission's deployment when we will better understand what that decision will imply.

In summary, this resolution defines the limited role to be played by our armed forces. It gives them a reasonable period to accomplish their mission. And it retains the prerogatives of Congress to pass judgment on the continued wisdom of this operation at a later date.

The chair simply wants to acknowledge that he has had some discussion with the ranking member on this. I think that Mr. Gilman has met with the minority caucus. I have met with the majority caucus. We recognize that in each of our caucuses there are differences of views.

We also recognize that the real determination of the final status of this resolution will be made on the floor of the House. So it is the intention of the chair, and I think of Mr. Gilman as well, and he can speak to that of course, that when we do go to the floor that we will urge the Speaker and the Rules Committee to provide—and we have reason to think that they will—all of the options, so that members will be able to vote for an early withdrawal, whatever that date may be, and I understand that might be determined at a later time by the Republican leadership, that they will be able to vote for no date at all. There are certainly members in our caucus on the Democratic side who favor no date at all.

And there will be an option, of course, to vote for a date on or about March 1. There may be other options as well. But I want to assure members that the chair has every reason to think that all of your options will be protected when you go to the floor, so that you will be able to vote however you think best for American policy at that point.

I also want to thank Mr. Gilman very much for his cooperation in working with this approach. The chair has tried to be responsive to his concerns here. And we have worked together to proceed in this manner. Mr. Gilman.

STATEMENT OF MR. GILMAN

Mr. GILMAN. Thank you, Mr. Chairman. Thank you for yielding, and thank you for the opportunity to try to work out some sort of an arrangement on the procedures of this bill.

Mr. Chairman, as you know, we first received this proposed Torricelli resolution late last night. It was first distributed to our minority members this morning.

Mr. Chairman, our minority, having met in caucus this morning, is firmly opposed to the adoption of this resolution. We oppose it both procedurally and substantively.

Our procedural objection is that the resolution was drafted virtually in private and withheld from the minority until almost the last minute. And a copy was provided to our minority staff only at about 7:30 p.m. last evening.

Accordingly, many of us first saw the resolution just a few hours ago, and simply had not enough time to carefully review and develop possible amendments to a resolution of this nature, one that includes the question of whether or not we should authorize a military operation in which American lives may be lost, which is probably the most solemn issue that can come before our committee.

Mr. Chairman, we would prefer postponing this measure for a mark-up to enable us to more fully digest the resolution. But because of the shortness of time, we will not offer any amendments today, nor will we make any more than a few observations about the substance of the resolution.

I expect that we will have amendments if the measure does reach the floor. I hope, Mr. Chairman, that you will support a rule making such amendments in order.

But I do suggest, Mr. Chairman, that the procedures which have been followed to date have been a disservice to the Congress and the American people. The American people have been demanding a full and careful debate and consideration of the President's policy in Haiti. While we all agree about trying to restore a democratically elected President in Haiti, we do differ about the extensiveness of military involvement. I regret that to date that we have not had such a debate on the House floor. Turning to the substance of the resolution, Mr. Chairman, I think that we owe it to our constituents to be frank about what this resolution is all about. It provides retroactive authorization for President Clinton's decision to launch a U.S. military occupation of Haiti.

Most of us are of the opinion that the President could have received congressional authorization in advance for his plan to occupy Haiti, something which we have been urging him to do. That may be why the President never really came to the Congress to seek out such an authorization.

But now, not having been made part of that decision by the administration to intervene, the proponents of this resolution want to try to bring Congress back into the picture by having us provide retroactive authorization of the President's action.

Some will say that it is congressional complicity and a gross foreign policy blunder by the administration, a blunder that is certain to cost hundreds of millions of dollars, and will cost American lives, and is questionable in any event about achieving its stated objectives.

This measure would require a congressional acquiescence to a policy that a significant majority of us believe to be wrong. Our constituents expect more of us than this kind of a resolution.

Undoubtedly, the argument will be made that even members who oppose military occupation of Haiti should support the resolution, because it does set a firm date of March 1, 1995 for winding down the U.S. occupation. For that, we commend Mr. Torricelli for trying to set a final date.

But, Mr. Chairman, this March 1 date actually is not any deadline. All that happens on March 1, according to this resolution, is that the authorization granted to the President by this resolution expires on that date. But the President already has our forces in Haiti without any authorization. He has made clear that he is comfortable relying on his constitutional authority to keep our forces there as long as he deems it necessary.

In other words, Mr. Chairman, and my colleagues, all that happens on March 1 is that the situation will revert to the one that exists today. If the President wants to keep our forces in Haiti beyond that date, he can and will do so. All this resolution does is to give the administration legal and political cover under the War Powers Act.

Let us remember what President Clinton had in mind in Haiti. He plans to keep 2,000 to 3,000 U.S. forces there as part of U.N. peacekeeping force until February of 1996. That is almost a year and a half from now. We recognize that the resolution contains expedited procedures which may allow us to vote on that plan sometime next spring.

Such an expedited procedure is a sound idea. But we question why the resolution postpones its availability until as late as next spring. Many of us would like to vote on the President's plan to extend the occupation into 1996 now rather than next spring.

It has been suggested that the U.N. peacekeeping force, which may be as much as 50 percent American in its composition or more, may be put under foreign command, but the resolution is silent on any foreign command of the U.N. led force.

These are just a few of some of our objections to this resolution, Mr. Chairman. It is not our intention to offer any amendments at this time. But we do reserve our opportunities to have our amendments considered when this measure reaches the floor. We will welcome your cooperation to that extent.

Accordingly, I urge my colleagues to oppose the adoption of this resolution. And I thank the chairman for yielding.

Chairman HAMILTON. The chair will recognize members who want to speak. But let me get the resolution in front of us. The Chief of Staff will report the resolution.

Mr. VAN DUSEN. H.J. Res. 416, "Providing limited authorization for the participation of U.S. Armed Forces in the multinational force in Haiti and providing for the prompt withdrawal of U.S. Armed Forces from Haiti."

Chairman HAMILTON. Without objection, further reading of the resolution is dispensed with and printed in the record in full.

[H.J. Res. 416 appears in appendix 1.]

Chairman HAMILTON. The chair recognizes the gentleman from New Jersey, Mr. Torricelli.

STATEMENT OF MR. TORRICELLI

Mr. TORRICELLI. Mr. Chairman, of all of the difficult and contentious issues that I can recall coming before this committee, this is among the most troublesome. There are many of us who believe that a long time ago this country learned a lesson, that our military forces should never be engaged in the field unless our people were united in purpose, and this Congress was fully supportive.

There are 17,000 young Americans now occupying a foreign nation without this Congress ever having had a debate, and against overwhelming opposition by the American people.

The approach that is now being followed in this committee in debating and adopting this resolution is not as I would have had it. There are few members of this committee who would have proposed this approach. It is, however, an attempt to deal with the reality of the situation.

Without this resolution, there is no congressional debate, and no procedures for a termination. And instead, the Congress is likely to be faced with a situation where there will be an attempt to end all appropriations immediately, or the policy goes forward with no control or congressional involvement.

This country and our soldiers deserve better. While I personally did not support intervention in Haiti, I would not support and believe that it is not fair to end without notification and simply remove all appropriations for young Americans while they are serving their country and deserve our support regardless of our beliefs about policy.

Nor do I believe that it is in the best interests of our constitutional government or in protecting the prerogatives of this institution to proceed without the Congress having debated and establishing some control over this policy.

Both the resolution before you and the scenario that Chairman Hamilton has outlined is an attempt to serve all of these objectives. And proceeding to the House with a March 1 deadline, and protecting the rights of Mr. Hastings to offer an amendment to remove the date consistent with his own interests and objectives, and for Mr. Gilman to offer a date significantly in advance of the March 1 deadline.

Speaking for the resolution itself, it does, however, offer a real opportunity to set a limit on both the scope and the details of the U.S. commitment, while offering the institution a chance after February 1 on an expedited basis to bring legislation to the floor to terminate the U.S. involvement, if that is the judgment of the Congress at that point.

It requires the President to submit three different reports on the cost, the scope, and the nature of U.S. involvement in the interim. The resolution specifically limits the scale of the U.S. involvement to the restoration of the democratic government, and providing security to that objective.

Therefore, the mission, both in its scale and the date, is well defined. I recognize that there are members who would have approached the issue differently. My own sentiments are no different than yours. But to fail to act is to have this Congress adjourn without debate in setting absolutely no limits on this involvement. I believe that would not be responsible.

I would urge my colleagues to have this resolution passed today in committee, and proceed to the Rules Committee. Mr. Hastings and Mr. Gilman can offer their alternative approaches. And before we adjourn and return to meet our constituents, we have a full, free and fair debate about this involvement in Haiti.

I believe that is the responsible approach, while being fair to our soldiers and indeed giving the President of the United States a full measure of support consistent with the kinds of controls we believe are in the national interest.

Thank you, Mr. Chairman.

Chairman HAMILTON. The chair has the following members who have indicated that they want to speak. On the minority side, Hyde, Roth, Smith, Bereuter, Rohrabacher, Manzullo, Royce, and Burton. And on the majority side, Engel, Menendez, Hastings, Johnston, McKinney, Wynn, and Payne. Mr. Hyde.

STATEMENT OF MR. HYDE

Mr. HYDE. Thank you very much, Mr. Chairman.

I want to congratulate Mr. Torricelli and you for bringing this resolution forward. It is a vehicle for us to study and to debate this very important issue. It is unfortunate that it comes so late. This situation, as distinguished from Grenada and Panama, which involved secrecy, speed, and American citizens, could have and should have been debated before we committed our troops to what may well be an insurmountable task, for which they are ill equipped, for nation building, restoration of democracy where there has never been a democracy despite the one event of the election, and developing an economy of a country that is certainly a basket case.

We do not want an open ended authority to tie our military down. Our military is increasingly being eviscerated by Congress and the administration. And therefore, it is good that this has a date of March 1.

My suggestion to Mr. Gilman and the Republicans would be that we accept the date of March 1, because we do not want to be charged with under-cutting or short circuiting the reasonable efforts of the administration to extricate ourselves from a situation that now we are there, that we need to be extricated from.

So I would urge that we accept the date of Mr. Torricelli, and assuming that is Mr. Hamilton's date, but that we put some teeth into it, rather this merely being an authorization which sits there and does nothing. That on March 1 that Mr. Gilman's resolution, which withdraws funds for this adventure, for this excursion, for this operation, be incorporated by way of an amendment into this resolution, so that it does withdraw our troops. And Congress asserts its power of the purse to withdraw funds for any further stay there. And at the date selected by Mr. Torricelli.

So I would think that is the proper resolution of this. And we can debate this on the floor. Again it is unfortunate that we did not have a chance to debate it earlier where the expressions of the American people as expressed through Congress would have been heard in opposition to this.

We, Republicans, and I daresay plenty of Democrats do not want to be associated with a retroactive authorization of something that they disapproved of and would not have authorized. And that is what is supporting this resolution as it is currently drafted does.

So for that reason, I am going to oppose this resolution, meanwhile again welcoming its selection of March 1. And instead of just ending the authority for us to be there, I would like to have our authority effectively terminated by withdrawing funds on that date.

And I thank the chairman for giving me this opportunity to express myself.

Chairman HAMILTON. Mr. Engel.

STATEMENT OF MR. ENGEL

Mr. ENGEL. Thank you, Mr. Chairman.

I rise in support of the resolution. And let me say that I substantially want to associate myself with much of the remarks of Mr. Torricelli. I think that Congress obviously needs to be consulted and to authorize going into Haiti. And I think that the administration should have come to Congress.

But I think that we also need to give credit where credit is due. And I think that it has been very fashionable these days to bash the President and bash every move that he makes in foreign policy, and criticize everything that he tries to do.

The fact of the matter is that credit should be given to the President. When the mission to Haiti was successful by former President Carter, and Colin Powell, and Senator Nunn, President Clinton was able to get an agreement whereby our troops could go into Haiti peacefully and occupy the country peacefully. I think that was a major breakthrough in diplomacy. President Clinton deserves tremendous credit for it.

You know, there is a dangerous attitude of isolationism in some circles in Congress, which I think is very, very dangerous. I have often said that foreign policy ought to be bipartisan. That it should not be used as a means of trying to get the President, or box him in, or humiliate him, or prove him wrong.

I think that there are times when America does have vital interests. We have vital interests in Cuba—we just passed a resolution about Cuba, because it is in our hemisphere. And when refugees leave Cuban shores, it affects us. And I think that the same is true for Haiti.

I do not think that we can continue to have a policy where refugees leave and want to come to our shores, and somehow we say, well, that somehow or other is not in America's vital interests. I think it is.

So we can quarrel over procedures, and we can quarrel over whether the President should have come to Congress. And as I said, he should have. But here we have a resolution before us which reasserts congressional control over the situation.

We can argue about a March 1 deadline. And frankly, I have some reservations over whether there ought to be a deadline at all. I think that the military certainly is opposed to a deadline. And there can be a case made to say that a deadline would give the enemies of democracy a chance to kind of hold out for a fixed date.

I think that we ought not to have a Somalia mentality here. What happened in Somalia was a terrible thing. But I do not think that we ought to use it as a base so that every time American troops are in potential hostility that we want to quickly set a date and urge the troops to come home.

I did not see a great clamor in some circles here, by some of my friends on the other side of the aisle, with Grenada and Panama, or the bombing of Libya, when Congress was not consulted at all, and there were Republican Presidents.

I think sometimes that the Commander in Chief has to do what he thinks is in the best interests of the country. We are here now, and we are debating a policy. There have been some charges for instance that American troops are somehow going to come under foreign command. If you read the resolution, that is not the case at all. American troops must always be under American command.

And I think again that we do have a stake in restoring democracy and human rights in Haiti. The United States has to have the credibility to say and do the things that we think are important in this hemisphere. Haiti is not very far from our shores. And what happens there does absolutely affect us.

So I think that this resolution is a good compromise. I am keeping my options open when Mr. Hastings makes his amendment on the floor. Because again I am very concerned about tying the hands of our military.

But let us conduct our foreign policy in a bipartisan fashion. Let us not attempt to use it to play politics, or to bring the President down. We have a resolution before us here. I think that it is a reasoned resolution. It is a compromise. It reasserts congressional control. It sets the March 1 deadline, and authorization would be needed to go beyond that deadline.

I think that this is fair, and I certainly support the resolution. Thank you, Mr. Chairman.

Chairman HAMILTON. Just so members know, I have had several inquiries about when we will vote. It is hard, of course, for the chair to estimate that. I do have 14 speakers who have requested to speak. Mr. Roth.

INQUIRY ON DATE FOR FLOOR CONSIDERATION

Mr. ROTH. Mr. Chairman, a question to the chair. I have an amendment, but I do not know if I want to offer it at this time. The question that I have for you is next week may be the last week that we are in session.

Do you have a commitment from the leadership that they are going to bring this up to the floor next week?

Chairman HAMILTON. Mr. Roth, I do not think that I have a commitment. I certainly have the expectation that they are fully planning on bringing this bill to the floor. I have never had any suggestion that they would not. But I cannot honestly say to you that I have a commitment. I have never asked them for one. I just assumed that it would move forward.

Mr. ROTH. And further, Mr. Chairman, when you go to the Rules Committee, did I understand you correctly, are you going to ask for an open rule?

Chairman HAMILTON. I did not say an open rule. I said that we would try to assure that members on the time question have all of their options in front of them. I am aware of three or four of those options now. Now there are other issues raised by this resolution other than the time certain. And my position would be that we ought to debate and have a rule that permits the major policy options. But I did not say an open rule.

STATEMENT OF MR. ROTH

Mr. ROTH. Thank you, Mr. Chairman.

Mr. Chairman, with respect to this resolution, I think that we in the Congress, as I read this resolution, are acquiescing much too easily. Basically, what we are doing here is saying hey, we were not there for the take off, but we are going to be there for the crash landing.

I remember as a youngster watching the Laurel and Hardy movies where Oliver Hardy used to say Stan Laurel, "Mr. President, that is another fine mess you got us into."

Haiti also reminds me of the movie of a tiny country declaring war on the United States and then surrendering to get foreign aid, "The Mouse that Roared." It was very humorous.

While Haiti is Bill Clinton's mouse that roared, it is no joke, this is reality. And the cost to the American taxpayer can only be expressed in one word, wow.

But do you know what upsets me most about this policy? It is the duplicity of it. We are now told that President Clinton is going to use $5 million. Stop and think about this. He is going to use $5 million of secret funds to facilitate Aristide's return.

Well, my friends, if this is a democracy in Haiti, and the people love Aristide so much, why has our CIA been down there spending millions of dollars, and why is the President using $5 million of secret funds, of taxpayer funds, to grease the skids for Aristide's return? I would like an answer to that.

Now I want the American people to know when they see the demonstrations in Haiti for Aristide that they may well be financed, yes, by your American tax dollars. Now if we are going to restore Aristide and we say that there is democracy in Haiti, to me that is real duplicity.

And then we wonder why the American people have no trust and confidence in their government or in their President. How can they?

Mr. HASTINGS. Would the gentleman yield?

Mr. ROTH. I would be happy to yield.

Mr. HASTINGS. I would just like to ask a question.

Do you have authority for the proposition that you set forth regarding the spending of $5 million?

Mr. ROTH. Yes, it was in the news this morning.

Mr. HASTINGS. The news?

Mr. ROTH. It was on public radio this morning, that the President is going to use $5 million to grease the skids for Aristide's return. And I take back the balance of my time to continue.

What we should be doing in this resolution is trying to save the troops from another Lebanon massacre and another Somalia disaster. We have here in this country Haiti where every leader since 1804, every leader since 1804, has either been deposed or has fled except for Papa Doc. There has not been democracy in Haiti.

But our President is risking the lives of American soldiers simply to try to save what is left of his tattered and torn credibility. Now the President is committing hundreds of millions of taxpayer dollars to this pointless fiasco.

And the Clinton policy in Haiti is destined to fail. The only question is how many Americans will be killed, and how much money will be squandered. Haiti has never been a democracy. The last time that we foolishly entered Haiti, we were stuck there for 19 years with nothing to show for it but dead Americans and dead Haitians.

As we sink further into this swamp, the same thing is going to happen. In Haiti, Bill Clinton has nowhere to go but down. Our troops should never have gone into Haiti. And the last time we should have learned a lesson to leave as quickly as possible.

Now when Christopher was before our Foreign Affairs Committee, he said that when the Clinton administration goes into a foreign country, there are four questions that have to be answered. One, what is the goal? Two, is there a reasonable chance for success? Three, does it have the backing of the American people? And four, how do we get out?

And these four questions have not been answered in this policy. And we as the Congress have an obligation to the American people, and we have to speak forthrightly. All of the Congressmen are going to scream after the crash landing. Now is the time to speak up. Now is the time to speak up, not when the crash landing takes place.

I thank the chairman for yielding.

Chairman HAMILTON. Mr. Menendez.

STATEMENT OF MR. MENENDEZ

Mr. MENENDEZ. Thank you, Mr. Chairman, very briefly. I intend to support the resolution as a vehicle to create a debate on the House floor, but my support now is in no way an indication of my intentions on this matter as to the different options that may be considered on the floor. But I do believe that this is a proper way to proceed, to have a debate. Whether it is finally had now versus when it could have been had.

The important part is that the debate does take place. And I believe that the resolution is a vehicle to accomplish that, and I will be supporting it.

Chairman HAMILTON. Mr. Smith.

STATEMENT OF MR. SMITH

Mr. SMITH. Thank you, Mr. Chairman.

Mr. Chairman, the debate and the vote on the invasion and occupation of Haiti should have occurred—and I think that members on both sides of the aisle agree with this—before and not after that invasion.

I would remind members that I had introduced a resolution, H. Con. Res. 264, on June 30 which would have configured a bipartisan congressional commission. The commission would have consisted of members of both sides, who would present possible policy options, and report back within 45 days. Had the resolution passed when it was introduced or soon thereafter, we would have had the product sometime in August, or at the latest in early September.

Unfortunately, the administration was very much against that. As a matter of fact, both in response to my own resolution and that which was proposed by Senator Dole, the administration lampooned the initiative as a dilatory tactic.

We wanted to have an honest, thought-provoking, incisive debate about Haiti and what the options were. We sought to mitigate the human rights abuses in Haiti, and facilitate democracy there, without imperiling the lives of Americans. We wanted to find a peaceful solution rather than a solution brought by the barrel of a gun.

Unfortunately, the administration shunted all of that aside, and accused us of delaying tactics. I can absolutely assure you that my intentions were not for delaying. They were to find a just solution to the crisis and the agony that is Haiti's.

I tried for several weeks as well, Mr. Chairman, to put together a delegation. We had responses from both Republican and Democratic members who wanted to go to Haiti, and meet with duly-elected members of their parliament, who like President Aristide, were elected in an authenticated election, approved by the Organization of American States. We were denied that opportunity to travel to Haiti.

Mr. GILMAN. Would the gentleman yield?

Mr. SMITH. I would be happy to yield.

Mr. GILMAN. And they invited us to come.

Mr. SMITH. Yes, they invited us. They wanted to find some common ground, parliament to parliament in recognition that they too are part of the governing body of Haiti—President Aristide and the duly-elected members of their parliament. And we found no cooperation from the State Department to facilitate that trip and obtain the necessary waiver from the U.N. Sanctions Committee.

Again, an attempt made in a bipartisan way to find a peaceful solution was put aside. Now we find ourselves faced with this resolution after the fact. I do thank my friend, Mr. Torricelli, for his well-meaning effort to set a day for withdrawal of U.S. Armed Forces from Haiti, although it remains an open question, whether or not the March 1 deadline is binding as drafted in the resolution.

Let me note for the record that my chief reservation about the pending resolution is its authorization of the use of U.S. Armed Forces to "stabilize" the security situation in Haiti, so that an orderly progress may be made in transferring the functions of government in that country to the democratically elected Government of Haiti.

It seems to me that the administration, even if this is binding, can find enough wiggle room and enough open endedness in that language to justify virtually anything that they might do in Haiti.

Let me just ask the administration, perhaps Secretary Sherman, to explain.

Chairman HAMILTON. The time of the gentleman has expired.

Mr. SMITH. I would ask permission to ask a question of the administration vis-a-vis this resolution.

Chairman HAMILTON. The gentleman asks unanimous consent to proceed for——

Mr. SMITH. Two minutes.

Chairman HAMILTON. For two additional minutes.

Is there any objection?

If not, you may proceed.

Mr. SMITH. I thank the chair and my colleagues.

I wish to ask some brief questions about the resolution, so that we know exactly where the administration stands.

One, does the administration believe that the authorization contained in the resolution is legally necessary to keep U.S. forces in Haiti?

Two, does the administration consider the March 1 date contained in the resolution to be legally binding; in other words, does it require the withdrawal of U.S. forces by that date?

And three, does the administration support this resolution?

Ms. SHERMAN.[4] Congressman, as you know, this administration, as other administrations, has disagreed with the Congress over who authorizes and whether the President is Commander in Chief of U.S. forces. And as your colleagues have pointed out, forces are in Haiti without prior authorization from the Congress. And this administration believes, as did virtually every other administration, including President Bush who prior to the Gulf War vote said that he felt that he had the authority to proceed whether or not Congress gave him the authority to do so, that the deployment was consistent with the President's authority as Commander in Chief.

So there has been an ongoing debate between the executive and legislative branch. So we, as other administrations, do take the position that the President as Commander in Chief can deploy U.S. forces as he has done in this case.

Nonetheless, we are quite well aware that if the Congress sets a deadline in a piece of legislation, that it has a tremendous political force. And it also sends signals to our troops on the ground and to both our friends and our enemies on the ground. And as in the letter that has come up with this morning from General Shalikashvili, Chairman of the Joint Chiefs of Staff, and Secretary Perry, and as you heard in open testimony yesterday at a hearing held by this committee, the administration does not support a fixed date.

We appreciate what the chairman is trying to do, and what Congressman Torricelli is trying to do, and what this committee is trying to do to bring about a debate on this issue. But we firmly oppose a fixed date.

Mr. SMITH. You said this resolution has tremendous political force.

But, the language in the resolution is not legally binding on the administration?

Ms. SHERMAN. The administration, as other administrations, takes the position that the President has the authority as the Commander in Chief to deploy forces. There will be disagreements about that, and the lawyers will probably be debating this, if this is enacted into law, for some time. But we certainly take it quite seriously.

Mr. SMITH. But there is no assurance that this has any legal effect on the administration?

Ms. SHERMAN. As I said, there has been long disagreement over this issue.

Chairman HAMILTON. Without objection, the letter to which Ms. Sherman refers, to the Speaker from the Chairman of the Joint

[4] Hon. Wendy Sherman is the Assistant Secretary of State for Legislative Affairs.

Chiefs of Staff and from the Secretary of Defense will be made part of the record.

[The letter appears in appendix 3.]

Chairman HAMILTON. Mr. Hastings.

STATEMENT OF MR. HASTINGS

Mr. HASTINGS. Thank you, Mr. Chairman.

Mr. Chairman, as most members of the committee know, I have been a consistent advocate of our involvement in Haiti and our intervention. And I have been an advocate even before coming to this Congress.

It is because I perceive myself as a supporter of democracy and as a humanitarian, and certainly as a resident of south Florida, I fervently wish to see this situation resolved. I said from day one that if Haiti is not hospitable to its own people, those same people will flock to south Florida. And we have seen with the recent influx of leaky boats that this is indeed the case.

Mr. Chairman, I do not advocate sending young Americans into a potentially dangerous situation carelessly or haphazardly. And nor am I a blind supporter of the Clinton administration with reference to the Haiti policy. On the contrary, I have been a constant critic of the administration. But I support the administration's policy on Haiti, because I support the concept of democracy in its purest institutions.

I listened to many members of this committee during the cold war lament the lack of democracy and democratic regimes around the world. And there is one little country in our own backyard that is screaming for our help to try to establish democracy.

Should we ignore their pleas, because the person who chose to throw out a life preserver is a President that some members of this committee and members of Congress want more than anything to embarrass?

A footnote right there, Mr. Chairman. It is ironic that we are here debating a successful occupation at this point. There has been extraordinary successes too numerous to mention without great prolixity.

I would pray that between now and March 1 that our forces will be able to stabilize the situation in Haiti without one single drop of American blood being shed. But I feel strongly that it is in the best interests of our troops to let their commanders decide when it is best for them to decide to return home.

Their future should be determined by what is best for them and the United States of America, rather than sordid election year politicking.

Mr. Chairman, I appreciate you very much, and Mr. Torricelli, and those who have been involved in the run up to this particular resolution. Today I support the resolution, and I most respectfully thank you for allowing me to reserve the option to offer an amendment at the appropriate time on the floor. I thank the chairman.

Chairman HAMILTON. Mr. Bereuter, and then Mr. Johnston. Mr. Bereuter.

STATEMENT OF MR. BEREUTER

Mr. BEREUTER. Mr. Chairman, I strongly oppose this resolution. The incursion into Haiti was haphazardly and incrementally conceived. It was ill begotten from the beginning, and it remains ill begotten policy. It is an illegitimate, improper, and ill advised incursion that we are involved in in Haiti.

I would have brought up the same language that Mr. Smith has already read from section 3. He points out to all of us here, and I say to my colleagues, that what we are doing is putting ourselves on line as authorizing the Haitian incursion in order to stabilize the security situation and to deliver humanitarian aid.

And I ask you if you really want to be involved in authorizing the Clinton administration to proceed with this ill begotten policy.

We have heard the obvious answer from Secretary Sherman that the end date, the get out date, in March was sent to the Congress only. It is not binding. I do not think that too many of us are going to disagree with that conclusion on her part. So what you are doing is putting yourself in line here and authorizing what was happening there.

I would say to my colleague, my friend, Mr. Engel, and say to Mr. Hastings that if you care to check the record, you will find that this objection is not partisan, and it is not aimed at embarrassing the President. If you check the record, you will find that this member and a couple of other members of Congress, who were trained as infantry officers or marines, objected strenuously to a Republican administration putting marines in a tactically indefensible position in Beirut Airport.

And I complained about that before the tragedy. I complained in the well of the House on at least two occasions. It was a proper use of military force, and I certainly lined up in support of the proper use of military force. But this was improper.

And I would have to say about the March 1 date, although well intended I am sure, I believe that a specific date is not a good idea. It establishes a set of circumstances that sometimes result in tragedy.

What this Congress should do before we leave is to pass a resolution which suggests that we should expeditiously get our members of the armed services out of Haiti consistent with their safety, at the earliest possible time consistent with their safety.

If we have a date like March 1, I am suggesting that it puts in play a variety of factors that we are not going to be happy about. And people are going to be waiting us out, and activities are going to take place between now and that date.

There is no proper end date. The important point is for us to say let us get our personnel out of there as expeditiously as we possibly can consistent with their safety. They do not belong there in the first place, and they ought to be pulled out.

Thank you, Mr. Chairman.

Chairman HAMILTON. Mr. Johnston, and then Mr. Rohrabacher.

STATEMENT OF MR. JOHNSTON

Mr. JOHNSTON. Thank you very much, Mr. Chairman.

Mr. Bereuter and I agree on the last part there that there should not be a date there. And I think that we also agree that they should get out as quickly as possible. And I appreciate his objectivity there.

The fact that he may have been against Lebanon though does not disregard the fact that this has become very partisan. I did not hear any debate against unilaterally invading Grenada or unilaterally invading Panama.

What we are doing is unprecedented in this century, if you go back. There was no drop dead date in Vietnam where half of the casualties occurred under the Nixon administration, more than under the Johnson or Kennedy administrations. There was no drop dead date on Saudi Arabia and Desert Storm where President Bush went in during the August recess with 500,000 troops without any congressional authority at all.

There was no drop dead date initially in Somalia where President Bush went in during the Christmas break. And when President Clinton was sworn in on January 20 of last year, there were 27,000 troops there. You know, when you talk about the fiasco of Somalia, that fiasco has got to be spread around among a lot of people.

Going back to Grenada and Panama, there are more Americans today in Haiti than there were in those countries combined, if you are talking about saving American lives.

Going back to the history of Haiti, the history of Haiti is that it was occupied under three Republican Presidents; Harding, Hoover, and Coolidge. So this stuff about foreign policy stopping at the shoreline I think is very embarrassing today. And I just think that we are embarking on something that is going to be tied around our necks in the future.

And if you listen to the people in the Defense Department, and if you listened to the professors yesterday and the open briefing today, they said the worst thing that we could possibly do is to have a drop dead date, that it is going to put our troops in peril. And I, like Congressman Hastings and Congressman Menendez, support this with a reservation that I will vote against it on the floor if it has a date certain in there.

Thank you, Mr. Chairman.

Chairman HAMILTON. Mr. Rohrabacher.

STATEMENT OF MR. ROHRABACHER

Mr. ROHRABACHER. Thank you very much, Mr. Chairman.

The professionals in our military who have spoken to this Congressman have opposed this operation as being a waste of their resources and a drain on resources that have been stretched to the breaking point.

If we keep committing our military personnel, at a time when we are decreasing military spending, by sending troops to Somalia, Rwanda, Haiti, or other countries which are not in the national security interest of the United States of America, we are not going to have the money and the resources available when our national security is really threatened in the future.

I just participated in the decommissioning of a Seabee reserve unit in my area of Orange County. The reason that this unit is

84-415 O - 94 - 4

being decommissioned is because we do not have the resources to keep it alive. We do not have those resources, because they are being wasted on nonsensical operations that have nothing to do with our security overseas.

Yes, Somalia did happen under the last administration. Yes, this Congressman was as opposed to that operation as he is opposed to this operation. There has been no explanation, a justified explanation, or any rational justification as to why Haiti is in the interest of the United States.

The bottom line is that most Americans believe and I certainly believe, as do most Members of Congress believe, that Haiti is not worth the loss of one American life. It is not in our national security interest.

What are we doing there? Maybe there is some sort of humanitarian impulse that is being satisfied. Maybe there are some political considerations that were given this by the White House before the decision was made, much more political consideration perhaps than we are making right now.

I would suggest this. Had the administration come to us and given us a chance to debate this and talk about it, things would have been different right now, and you would not have had to risk any American lives by saying oh, there is going to be a drop dead date, and thus it is going to put our people at risk.

I believe that the consensus throughout the Congress today is that those troops should be withdrawn. I know that this is the consensus throughout my congressional district, and I imagine throughout other people's congressional districts. It was a mistake for the President to send those troops into Haiti. They should be withdrawn at the earliest possible moment consistent with their own safety.

In terms of our discussions about the cold war, let me just note this. That there was an emergency situation in Grenada. American lives were at risk. Today, however, nobody is suggesting that the American lives in Haiti are at risk. I would, too, say that there was a lot of partisan attacks on the President after the military operation in Grenada as well.

What gets me is we have so many of the same people, that were opposed to any type of assistance for other countries that were fighting Communist aggression during the cold war and would not permit us to offer assistance, now supporting American intervention—the use of American troops abroad.

There is nothing inconsistent with saying that during the cold war when U.S. national security was at stake that we should somehow help those countries being threatened by a Communist takeover. But, I never advocated that a number of U.S. troops be sent into El Salvador.

Chairman HAMILTON. The time of the gentleman has expired.

Mr. ROHRABACHER. And I would suggest to you that that would have been a mistake then, and this is clearly a mistake now.

Chairman HAMILTON. Ms. McKinney, and then Mr. Manzullo.

STATEMENT OF MS. MCKINNEY

Ms. MCKINNEY. Thank you, Mr. Chairman.

I would like to join with my colleagues, Mr. Hastings, Mr. Bereuter, and Mr. Johnson, and say that, as you know, I am opposed to any legislation that sets a date certain. I would just like to say that we have already seen the benefits of the American presence. The Haitian parliament has begun the process of legislating an amnesty. The weapons buy back program is working. Human rights abuses are diminishing. The police and armed forces are on notice that atrocities will not be tolerated, and civil order is being restored.

President Aristide continues to underscore his commitment to peace, reconciliation, and national unity, and for free and fair elections. The Haitian people have been dying for democracy and now we have an opportunity to correct some of the mistakes that we have made in the past, and to help set that nation on the course for democracy. I will vote for this resolution, but I will support Representative Hastings on the floor.

Chairman HAMILTON. Mr. Manzullo.

STATEMENT OF MR. MANZULLO

Mr. MANZULLO. Thank you, Mr. Chairman.

I am very much disturbed over not only the timing of this resolution, but the wording of it. With regard to the timing, we are voting on a date to get out, but never had the opportunity to vote on whether or not to go in in the first place.

Second of all, as Mr. Smith from New Jersey pointed out, on page 3, section 3A, it says, "The U.S. armed forces are authorized to provide, participate, and lead the U.S. led forces in Haiti." In other words, this is a retroactive authorization and approval of what the President has done.

But more disturbing, Mr. Chairman, is the fact that on page 4, section 2, it talks about prohibition on foreign command. It says, "U.S. armed forces described in Subsection [a] shall remain under the command and control of officers of the U.S. armed forces at all times."

Now paragraph [a] in section 3, only applies to the present incursion of U.S. Armed Forces and supposedly bringing the country into stability. However, section 2 talks about transferring the operations in Haiti from the U.S. led force in Haiti to the U.N. led force in Haiti.

We are going to be in the same position where American troops are under the command of a conciliatory Danish general in Macedonia. This resolution is silent in terms of once the U.S. forces turn over operations to the U.N., whether or not the U.N. would be in charge of the rest of the operation.

Mr. Chairman, finally, this resolution again is indicative of the voodoo diplomacy of the Clinton administration's Haiti policy. We were told yesterday by Deputy Secretary of State Strobe Talbott that Mr. Aristide had been given a "bum rap."

The American people should be aware of the fact that he is a defrocked Roman Catholic priest, who was thrown out of his order because of his belief in violence. This is the man who while President replaced the entire Supreme Court of Haiti, and many mayors in that particular country. He replaced the Supreme Court without getting the permission of the parliament, and it was the parliament's job to give him permission.

And third of all, this is the man who in his autobiography on page 196 stated his love affair with Che Guevara, who was Castro's hatchet man.

To place American troops in harm's way to restore democracy led by a man like this is wrong.

But most of all, Mr. Chairman, this joint resolution leaves open the door for U.N. control, for a commander outside of the United States to lead the U.N. forces. Will that commander be from Antigua, the Bahamas, Barbados, Belize, Grenada, Jamaica, or Trinidad and Tabago? Or perhaps it will be from Russia, because Mr. Yeltsin has offered to send troops there also.

Chairman HAMILTON. Mr. Wynn, and then Mr. Royce. Mr. Wynn.

STATEMENT OF MR. WYNN

Mr. WYNN. Thank you, Mr. Chairman. I will be brief.

I understand that this resolution is designed to preserve all of the options that reflect the various points of view of the members of this committee and the members of Congress. And to that end, I intend to support it.

Personally, I would subscribe more closely to the views expressed by Deputy Secretary Deutsch yesterday to the extent that it is probably militarily unwise to telegraph to your opposition when you intend to leave.

Notwithstanding that though, Mr. Chairman, my concern is that we not set a date prematurely. There is some merit, I believe, to the arguments that a date certain gets us out of what many consider to be an intractable situation.

My point is simply this, Mr. Chairman. That if we are going to set a date certain, it should not be done until after we have achieved our one clear objective. And that is the transition of government from the military coup leaders to the democratically elected government of President Aristide.

I feel very strongly that if a date is to be set, that we ought to wait until Mr. Cedras steps down. Because it seems to me, particularly given his past pattern, that if we say that we are going to be out February 1 or March 1, that he will find some excuse for remaining in place, and therefore we would not have accomplished even our most fundamental objective. Or we will be faced with a situation where U.S. troops are forced into a much more aggressive posture in order to accomplish our stated initial objective of having him step down.

So if we were to exercise a little temperance and perhaps wait until after October 15, in which case he would have stepped down, then it certainly would make more sense to set a date certain in those circumstances.

So I would just note that for the committee, that I do intend to support the resolution.

SCHEDULING OF ADDITIONAL MARKUP SESSION

Chairman HAMILTON. The chair makes the following announcement. After consulting with Mr. Gilman, the chair wishes to notify members that we will have a short mark-up tomorrow at 10 a.m.

to take up resolutions on which floor action would be expected next week.

Mr. ACKERMAN. Mr. Chairman——

Chairman HAMILTON. That includes two——

Mr. ACKERMAN. Mr. Chairman, could we have a discussion on this before this is set?

Chairman HAMILTON. You are suggesting that it is not ready to come forward?

Mr. ACKERMAN. That is correct.

Chairman HAMILTON. OK. Then we will cancel this notification. I will ask that the members who are involved in these two resolutions on Vietnam, insofar as the chair knows they are Mr. Gilman, Mr. Ackerman, Mr. Rohrabacher, and Mr. Leach, to see if they can reach some kind of an accord before tomorrow morning.

Mr. GILMAN. Mr. Chairman, that is the first I knew that we were not prepared to move forward.

Is there some substantive problem?

Chairman HAMILTON. The chair would just ask that the members involved discuss it.

Mr. Royce is recognized, and then Mr. Payne. Mr. Royce.

EXTENDING PROHIBITION ON FOREIGN COMMAND OF U.S. FORCES

Mr. ROYCE. Yes, Mr. Chairman. I would ask unanimous consent to address a question to the author of the resolution, Mr. Torricelli, if I could.

Chairman HAMILTON. To Mr. Torricelli?

Mr. ROYCE. Yes. And the reason for that, Mr. Chairman, is that Mr. Engel made a statement that American troops will not be under foreign command. He said that if you read the resolution that you will notice that American troops will not be under—under U.N. command, he said.

Now this is very curious, because this is the opposite of the reading that our staff had of the bill. Of course, our staff points out that the President would like to have up to 3,000 U.S. forces in a U.N. led force in Haiti. And their feeling was that this might be a ruse. So let me just ask this question forthrightly.

Does this resolution prohibit foreign command of U.S. troops under a United Nations led peacekeeping force in Haiti? That is my question.

Mr. TORRICELLI. The resolution deals with the presence of U.S. forces under U.S. command until there is a transfer of authority of the operation to the United Nations. After March 1, if this is adopted and complied with by the President, presumably this operation changes to become from the U.S. occupation to the U.N. peacekeeping forces.

The judgment at that point about whether or not the United States participated in that force and who would command it is entirely independent of this resolution. This resolution deals solely with the issue of U.S. occupation of Haiti until the March 1 deadline. Passing this or not passing it does not impact the U.N. question.

Mr. ROYCE. In light of that, then Mr. Engel might want to reread this resolution and understand what it really states. And I would ask a second question.

Mr. ENGEL. Would the gentleman yield, since he mentioned my name?

Mr. ROYCE. Yes.

Mr. ENGEL. I would ask the gentleman to look at the bottom of page 3 when it says limitations and termination of authorization, "The authorization provided shall expire March 1, 1995." And at the top of page 4 it says, "Prohibition on foreign command. The U.S. armed forces described in Subsection [a] shall remain under the command and control of officers of the U.S. armed forces at all times."

So what Mr. Torricelli said is absolutely true. This talks about American troops being under the command of Americans, and it talks about until March 1. And it does not address what happens after March 1 when the United Nations takes over. But this does not influence it in any way.

Mr. ROYCE. Then my question to the author would be would you be open to friendly amendments when we reach the floor, which would extend the prohibition on foreign command of U.S. Armed Forces to U.N. led American forces in Haiti? That is my question.

Mr. TORRICELLI. In answer to your question, and this actually goes to several questions that were asked, I believe that it is somewhat disingenuous of the administration to argue that there is a danger to American forces by setting a deadline, when the administration recognizes that after the U.S. occupation forces leave that there is going to be a United Nations peacekeeping force.

Therefore, international presence and security forces are not leaving Haiti. And there is no inherent advantage in people attacking our forces or creating incidents when they already know when we are leaving, but another force is going to remain in occupation.

I believe that Mr. Engel has answered accurately the question of while there is a U.S. occupation force that it is solely under U.S. command. But I would remind the gentleman that there is also a provision where after February 1 under expedited procedures that this Congress can deauthorize any U.S. presence after that date.

Therefore, the gentleman, and indeed any member of the institution, can file a request to have the United States to have no further presence after February 1. So if the gentleman's concern is after March 1, there is a continued presence, and it would be under foreign command. Under this resolution, the gentleman has the option of ending that potential.

Mr. ROYCE. Then, Mr. Chairman, if I could ask one last question.

And that would simply be unanimous consent to call up Assistant Secretary Sherman to ask her if the administration could give this committee assurance today that the U.N. led force in Haiti would be under the command and control of an American officer?

Ms. SHERMAN. Congressman, that question was asked of Deputy Secretary Talbott and Deputy Secretary Deutsch yesterday at the hearing. And their answer was that we have every expectation that it will be a U.S. commander. I think that I should also hasten to say here, because it is very important and this is an issue that has been debated in the Congress in the past, that it is my understanding that the armed services, and the President, Secretary Perry, and the Chairman of the Joint Chiefs always maintain a chain of command where our forces always ultimately are under the command and control of the U.S. chain of command to the President under any circumstances.

But the actual commander is being worked out with the U.N., but it is our expectation that it will be a U.S. commander. And that is what they said yesterday which I am delighted to repeat today.

Chairman HAMILTON. Mr. Payne. And he will be followed by Mr. Burton. Mr. Payne.

STATEMENT OF MR. PAYNE

Mr. PAYNE. Thank you very much, Mr. Chairman.

As you probably know, I am one who supports the President wholeheartedly in his actions. As I indicated at one of the other hearings, I had the privilege to get at the United Nations when President Clinton gave his address to the United Nations on Monday.

And during the break following that and the reception that evening, the comments were the United States is resolved, and the fact that the President stayed the course. And the action of the U.S. military was one that was discussed by many nations around the world that the United States of America was looked at in a proud and dignified manner.

I would also say that we are throwing around terms that I question whether they are appropriate, when we talk about an occupation force. I question whether the U.S. military now or under the U.N. is going to be considered an occupation force.

I also heard the word "blunder" used as it talked about our intervention into Haiti. I think that you could not have had an introduction of troops in a more orderly manner. And if that is considered a blunder, I do not understand that word.

The fact that we have troops in other countries seems to be a revelation to some members. In South Korea, we have tens of thousands of troops. And when we are talking about the remaining 2,000 troops in Haiti perhaps after March, April, or May, when we hear people talking about U.S. troops being in a foreign country, in Europe we have had tens of thousands of troops, and throughout the world. So it is really not a new policy for U.S. troops to be on foreign soil.

I would just like to say that none of us want to see, and we hope that there is not loss of American lives. We hope that everything could work without any casualties. But we know that in the real world that these things do not always occur.

But I was just reminded that it was decided that we would use the U.S. military in fighting fires on the West Coast. And you may recall tragically about 4 or 5 months ago or 3 or 4 months ago that 19 local fire fighters died in a battle to control the fires in that region. And it is unfortunate.

So when we look at situations where people have difficulties, you can never say that there will not be a casualty anywhere. So I would just like to say that our resolve—in Grenada, there were 350 Americans, and in Haiti there are over 3,000 Americans.

So when we compare these things together, we hope that all will work well. The parliament is meeting today. I am proud of the job that our servicemen are doing. And I think that we should support them 100 percent.

Thank you, Mr. Chairman.

Chairman HAMILTON. Mr. Burton, and then Mr. McCloskey. Mr. Burton.

STATEMENT OF MR. BURTON

Mr. BURTON. Mr. Chairman, thank you.

I would just like to ask the Secretary, Secretary Sherman, if she would respond in writing to the question posed by the gentleman from New Jersey, Mr. Smith, regarding whether or not it is binding for us to set a date certain for us to get our troops out of there. We would like to have that in writing, not just your statement for the record.

[The information follows:]

If enacted, the resolution would have provided explicit congressional authorization for U.S. Armed Forces to participate in the U.S.-led force in Haiti until March 1, 1995. It would not, by its terms, have required the withdrawal of U.S. forces by March 1.

Mr. BURTON. I would like to set the record straight on Grenada. I went down to Grenada right after the invasion. And the Democratic leadership was doing everything they could to undermine what the President had done. There is just no question about that, and the record would reflect it.

In addition to that, on November 1, 1983, the House approved a resolution that we would get our forces out of Grenada within 90 days, and that is a matter of record.

The other thing is that it was indicated that there was no real threat to human life. I want you to know that there were 500-plus students at that medical college down there that literally got off the plane and kissed U.S. soil, because they thought that their lives were in jeopardy. That they were held hostage by Mr. Bishop and the Communist Grenadan Government. So this is not the same situation as that which we faced in Grenada in 1983.

Now let me just say this. President Clinton did not talk to the Congress, and he did not ask the opinion of the American people, even though probably 75 to 80 percent of the Congress and the people did not want this invasion to take place. But he did talk to the United Nations, and he asked their support for a resolution in the Security Council.

Now my question is why in the world is the President going to the Security Council instead of the people of the United States through their elected representatives? It shows a disdain I think for this body. And I think that every one of us, Democrats and Republicans, should be concerned about that.

We had a dubious policy in Somalia. Granted that the troops were sent into there under a Republican who was going to get them out in a very short period of time. But that period of time was extended. And after it was extended by President Clinton, the Secretary of Defense, Les Aspin, would not allow M–1, or A–1 tanks, or armored personnel carriers there. And as a result, it took us 12½ hours to go across Mogadishu to try to save 17 marines who were downed in a helicopter, and they were killed. And we witnessed one of them being dragged through the streets naked.

The American people do not want a replay of that, because of our ineptness as a government, and because we are in a place where we should not be.

Now the President has not listened before, and I do not think that he is going to listen now. But I think that we ought to be very, very concerned about where we are going with this. It does not have the backing of the American people. The American people want those troops out of there now. Not 6 months from now, and not a year from now. And most certainly, they do not want American troops put under foreign command.

And if you do not believe that, go back to your home districts and ask your constituents. They do not want our troops under foreign command. And there is no guarantee that I have heard yet today that that will not take place. I want an ironclad guarantee that we are not going to have some hair brain down there running American forces around over Haiti.

And I would just like to say that the gentleman that we are putting back in power down there is no democrat. He does not believe in democracy and human rights. And if you do not believe that, look at his record. The gentleman down here just a few moments ago cited many of his past performances and his record.

And what we are doing is risking American lives for no good reason because we do not have any national interest down there. We should bring our troops home as quickly as possible, faster than March 1. And I am very concerned that we are going to keep them there much longer, and we are going to see a lot of them get killed or maimed unnecessarily.

The American people do not want it, and the Congress does not want it. Let us bring them home. It is not in our national interest to keep them there. And this resolution I do not think is going to solve the problem, even though I have great respect for Mr. Torricelli.

Chairman HAMILTON. Mr. McCloskey, and then Mrs. Meyers. Mr. McCloskey.

STATEMENT OF MR. MCCLOSKEY

Mr. MCCLOSKEY. Thank you very much, Mr. Chairman. I will try to be brief. I guess that nearly everything has been said, but not all of us are on the record saying it, to paraphrase one of our distinguished predecessors. I have great respect for Mr. Burton, but I really do not agree with him very much on a percentage basis. But, on some things, I do.

I think that the President did fail in not consulting with the Congress and the American people more in building the case for invasion. And particularly, I did press very much and argued for an authorizing vote, even if that possibly could have gone against the President. But I sincerely do think that overall that the administration has a very rational and justified policy as far as the stakes in Haiti and the concerns in Haiti.

And I might say in passing also that I am a little bit concerned about the oft recurring phrase, and I hear it in my district, that all of Haiti is not worth one American life. But I would like to think that lives are of infinite value, both Haitian and American. No one wants an American killed.

There are recent reports that U.S. troops have opened up some of the Cedras prisons, Mr. Chairman, with political prisoners there with their backs flayed open. I would like to have someone ask them and their families if the American effort is respected and appreciated. There are problems and challenges there as to regional stability. You cannot say that the refugees coming up onto the shores of Florida and potentially destabilizing that State's economy are of no concern to us.

And most particularly you cannot say that the human rights concerns in Haiti as to what is happening to thousands of poor and innocent human beings are inconsequential.

Mr. ROHRABACHER. Would the gentleman yield for a question?

Mr. MCCLOSKEY. No. I would like to finish, and then I will yield given the chairman's pleasure.

I appreciate very much the administration's concerns as to a date certain. I would prefer at this time, although I will be open to the arguments on the floor, that we leave this up to the administration, particularly to such people as General Shalikashvili. I would hope that my colleagues consult with—and I do not know what the answer would be—people like Colin Powell as to what that distinguished general in this case thinks of a date certain.

We need greater U.N. funding and commitment. We need a peaceful transfer of military troops and resources there, if you will. And it is a very volatile time with an election a matter of weeks away. Careers can rise or fall on what happens hundreds of miles or more away in Haiti. But this is no time for politics. There was no bashing.

There was no bashing of Reagan when he went into Grenada with no consultation, and no talk of American interests. We should give the President of the United States the same respect. We should give the President strong backing, not vitriolic criticism.

I thank you, Mr. Chairman.

Chairman HAMILTON. The chair will just say that we have four remaining speakers. Mrs. Meyers, Mr. Fingerhut, Ms. Cantwell, Mr. Faleomavaega. Mrs. Meyers.

STATEMENT OF MRS. MEYERS

Mrs. MEYERS. Mr. Chairman, thank you.

I oppose this resolution. The President did not come to Congress before his intended invasion, and we should not retroactively reauthorize now what Congress would not have authorized then.

But that is done. And a previous speaker indicated that we should pass this resolution to support the troops. But last week, this House voted to support the troops. So there is absolutely no question about that.

Finally, the resolution is ambiguous. It reads that the authorization expires on March 1. But on line 13, it is obvious that that pertains to U.S. led forces only. And we will have 3,000 to 4,000 troops there under U.N. command after that time with no final authorization date at all.

I oppose the resolution, Mr. Chairman. And I would yield for 1 minute to my colleague, Mr. Burton.

HUMAN RIGHTS VIOLATIONS IN HAITI

Mr. BURTON. I would just like to say to my colleague from Indiana that he did not read the newspapers. Because Michael Barnes, who was chairman of the Western Hemisphere Subcommittee, wrote a very spurious article about the invasion of Grenada. The Speaker of the House during the invasion of Grenada, Mr. O'Neill, took issue with it.

And even after they did criticize the President roundly, we did accept, both sides of the aisle, a 90-day limitation on the troops, and we did get them out of there.

Mr. MCCLOSKEY. Mr. Burton, will you yield?

Mr. BURTON. I have the time, do I not, Mr. Chairman?

Chairman HAMILTON. Yes.

Mr. BURTON. Regarding the whipping and the human rights violations in Haiti, let me just say that the President is going back there, Mr. Aristide. And Mr. Aristide has advocated publicly on numerous occasions putting a tire filled with gasoline around people's necks and burning them to death after tying their hands behind them.

Now tell me, is that worse than whipping? We are not putting a democrat, a human rights person, back in power. This guy is a bad apple, and we are risking American troops to do it. So do not give me that human rights baloney, because it will not wash.

I thank the gentle lady for yielding.

Chairman HAMILTON. Mr. Fingerhut.

STATEMENT OF MR. FINGERHUT

Mr. FINGERHUT. Thank you, Mr. Chairman.

It strikes me that the productive nature of this debate may be winding down. But it is important I think for those of us to put on record our votes and our reasons for voting as we do. I do not agree with our policy in Haiti and would not, had I had the opportunity to vote, have voted to support the mission.

However, it is clear to me, as the chairman stated, that once American troops are on the ground that the Congress of the United States is involved, must become involved, and ought to have the right to speak on this issue.

This committee, while we have profound responsibilities with respect to the House of Representatives' position on foreign affairs ought not to presume to speak for the House as a whole. What the chairman and the sponsor of this resolution have done is frame a resolution that we can present to the House, so that the House can work its will.

On that basis, I will support the resolution in the committee today, although my own personal views on this resolution will be expressed in greater detail when we do reach the floor.

I would add that I also take the chairman's assurance, as his word is always good, that with respect to the Rules Committee handling of this resolution, that it will attempt to structure the debate in such a way so that all of those of us on the committee who have a variety of viewpoints will be able to express those views, as will our colleagues not on this committee, when it comes to the House.

So I thank the chairman and the sponsor for framing this resolution for debate on the floor. I will support it, solely to get it to the floor.

Chairman HAMILTON. Ms. Cantwell.

STATEMENT OF MS. CANTWELL

Ms. CANTWELL. Thank you, Mr. Chairman.

Just as every member of this committee or almost every member of this committee has sought recognition to speak on this issue, I believe that the members of the full body also deserve that same opportunity. That is why I support the Torricelli resolution today.

If you are looking for more clarity in U.S. policy, this is at least a beginning. Not only in the policy area of saying bring our troops home as soon as possible, but in various reporting periods, authorization, and a termination date.

You may not agree with this termination date, as well as I have concerns about this termination date, and will be looking at various alternatives offered on the floor, this is the vehicle that we have before us now. If we want this fully debated, if we want to send a message that we have concerns, and that Congress wants to participate, then move the Torricelli resolution forward, so that all of our colleagues and the American people can fully have this issue debated.

Thank you, Mr. Chairman.

Chairman HAMILTON. The chair has Mr. Faleomavaega and Mr. Ackerman remaining. I think I have covered everybody. Mr. Faleomavaega.

STATEMENT OF MR. FALEOMAVAEGA

Mr. FALEOMAVAEGA. Thank you, Mr. Chairman.

I certainly want to commend the gentleman from New Jersey for offering this joint resolution with your support.

Mr. Chairman, as you are aware, I raised the question of a time table that the President intends to maintain our military presence in Haiti. And I asked Under Secretary Talbott yesterday specifically whether the 60-day requirement under the War Powers Resolution runs with some 19 days now since the President ordered our forces to be in Haiti.

As you know, the administration's response was they will get back to us. There was some uncertainty in the administration's position on this issue. And this bothers me, Mr. Chairman, because I reflect that there was also a resolution that we did some years ago. It was called the Gulf of Tonkin resolution. I do not think that there is any question in anybody's mind that the last thing that we ever want to do is to enter a protracted war like we did in Vietnam. And I do not think that it was ever the intention of the administration. And I pray to God, certainly not in the Congress.

Mr. Chairman, I can appreciate the President's concerns that he has got to be given some sense of flexibility in handling this critical issue. The lives of our men and women in the armed services and U.S. civilians are at stake. There are the tremendous problems of logisticals and the movement of forces is not a very easy task by any means.

At the same time, Mr. Chairman, the law is firm concerning the limitations placed upon the Presidential authority to use military forces. Beyond the 60-day grace period, I believe, the resolution now before us adequately addresses the concerns of the Congress. And it still leaves open in principle at least in my understanding the option for the President to come before the Congress to justify himself and his foreign policy concerning Haiti.

Now within that context, Mr. Chairman, I support the proposed resolution now before the committee.

Chairman HAMILTON. Mr. Ackerman.

STATEMENT OF MR. ACKERMAN

Mr. ACKERMAN. Thank you, Mr. Chairman.

I suppose that it might be interesting to note that one of the products that Haiti has historically had, has been baseballs for the American and National Leagues of our country, and there does not seem to be much need of that right now.

I think that it is also interesting to note how partisan we can suddenly get when it comes to protecting democracy for a bunch of people whose skins are darkly colored in comparison to how nonpartisan we can be when it comes to preserving democracy for a bunch of other people whose skins are lighter and provide us with our gasoline and our oil.

RACIAL FACTOR IN DEBATE ON HAITI INTERVENTION

Mrs. MEYERS. Mr. Chairman.

Mr. ACKERMAN. I reserve the balance of my time.

Mrs. MEYERS. Would the gentleman yield?

Chairman HAMILTON. Does the gentleman yield to the gentlewoman from Kansas?

Mr. ACKERMAN. I would be glad to yield.

Chairman HAMILTON. The gentlewoman.

Mrs. MEYERS. Mr. Chairman, I really resent that remark about partisanship and dark skins. I really think that Presidents, this one and the past one, have indicated that when we go into an area that it should be to solve a problem that is resolvable. That we should know what our goal is, and we should have a way in and a way to get out. And we should be able to do something effective while we are there.

We have not gone into Bosnia. We have not gone into other areas where the skins were light. And I think that is really an inappropriate thing to say.

Chairman HAMILTON. The chair recognizes——

Mr. ACKERMAN. Just reclaiming my time for a second. I am one who supported President Reagan. I am one who supported President Bush. I am one who is supporting our President right now, although I thought his initial policy was rather ill advised. I think that we ought not have gone in. I think that better consultation should have taken place with this Congress.

But I think that when we take a look at what resources the people have to bear on the system, that we suddenly jumped right in there on the Persian Gulf protecting what was the 68th province supposedly when we went in to save Kuwait, I think that the handwriting is pretty clear. I think people's points of views are colored.

I think that this issue, although there is a lot of gray, that there is also too much black and white involved. And I think that there is partisanship here when it comes to forming ranks behind the President.

Mr. GILMAN. Would the gentleman yield?

Mr. SMITH. Would the gentleman yield on that?

Chairman HAMILTON. Mr. Ackerman has the time.

Mr. SMITH. Would the gentleman yield?

Mr. ACKERMAN. I would be glad to yield.

Mr. SMITH. Now I have to join in and say that I, too, resent that comment. There has been no partisanship. We have tried before this became an issue to make this a bipartisan issue, which would essentially provide cover for the President. Most importantly, though, before any plans of this invasion or occupation occurred, we tried to come up with nonviolent solutions to Haiti.

If you look at the resolution that I introduced, it had equal representation of Democrats and Republicans on a congressional commission that would seek answers, and would go to Haiti to try to find answers. There is no partisanship here.

Mr. GILMAN. Would the gentleman yield?

Mr. ACKERMAN. There is no partisanship on your part, Chris, that is for sure.

Mr. GILMAN. Would the gentleman yield?

Chairman HAMILTON. Does the gentleman yield to Mr. Gilman?

Ms. MCKINNEY. Would the gentleman yield to me?

Mr. ACKERMAN. I would be glad to yield to the gentle lady.

Ms. MCKINNEY. Thank you. I would just like to commend the gentleman from New York for having the courage to say what many of us have felt all along. So I would just also like to associate myself with the words of the gentleman from New York, the very strong words.

Chairman HAMILTON. The time of the gentleman from New York has expired. The chair recognizes Mr. Gilman.

Mr. GILMAN. Mr. Chairman, I, too, join my colleagues in resenting making this a racial issue. Go back to Somalia, go back to the Persian Gulf, go back to any hostility, we have raised the War Powers Resolution time and time again. Regrettably, each administration has refused to accept the importance of the War Powers Resolution that the Congress has adopted.

I am sure that the gentleman from New York recognizes that most of us see the problem of trying to return a democratically elected President to his sovereignty. We all want to find the best resolution for that.

But in like manner, we also want to make certain that we are not doing anything to defeat the purpose of the War Powers Resolution, to allow the Congress to have the last say on whether or not we are going to be engaged in any hostility. Putting a color picture to all of this, a racial picture, does a disservice to the debate.

Mr. ACKERMAN. Will the gentleman yield?

Mr. GILMAN. Yes, I would be pleased to yield to the gentleman.

Mr. ACKERMAN. Which democratically elected leader did we restore in Kuwait, did I miss something?

Mr. GILMAN. Apparently, you missed the aggression by an overpowering nation trying to defeat a smaller nation.

Mr. ACKERMAN. I did not miss it at all.
Mr. GILMAN. That is what brought us to the issue.
Mr. ACKERMAN. I was very supportive of our President.
Mr. BURTON. Would the gentleman yield from New York?
Mr. GILMAN. I would be pleased to yield.
Mr. BURTON. Let me just say that I am the senior Republican on Africa. And I want to say that we have supported efforts in Angola. You may not have agreed with it, but we supported efforts in Angola. We have supported efforts in Zaire. We supported efforts in Mozambique. We supported efforts in the Sudan. In the Sudan where there is all kinds of oppression, racial oppression going on. We supported Ethiopia. We did support Somalia, although we did not like the way that it was handled. So do not give us that stuff that we are racist.
Mr. ACKERMAN. I do not remember going into Ethiopia.
Chairman HAMILTON. The gentleman from New York has the time. Mr. Gilman.
Mr. DIAZ-BALART. Would the gentleman yield?
Mr. GILMAN. I would be pleased to yield to the gentleman from Florida.
Mr. DIAZ-BALART. I thank the ranking member.
I would ask the gentleman from New York, as the consequences of his most unfortunate comment, that if those Democrats who criticized President Reagan for liberating Grenada were racists?
Mr. TORRICELLI. Mr. Chairman.
Chairman HAMILTON. The chair recognizes Mr. Torricelli to close debate.

STATEMENT OF MR. TORRICELLI

Mr. TORRICELLI. Mr. Chairman, before calling the question, I would like to again thank Mr. Gilman and Mr. Smith for their cooperation to bring this to this point, particularly my friend Alcee Hastings, who has been particularly cooperative in allowing the committee to proceed, and in allowing the full House to reach its own judgment.

I recognize that there are strong feelings on all sides of this issue. No question could be more important to members of this committee than dealing with the life and death of our armed forces, and the life of an entire people of a nation.

We have each in the balance, while protecting the prerogatives of the institution and the constitutional workings of our Government. At any time, that is a great number of issues to be considered. With a nation so divided and this Congress having been absent from the debate to date, it becomes particularly difficult.

In closing the discussion today, I simply want to briefly return to a pivotal question in the resolution raised by Mr. Smith earlier. And that is, does what we do here today have real meaning. Secretary Sherman provided a legal answer to Mr. Smith's legal questions.

I want to close the debate by providing a matter of policy. Because what we intend to do here today should have real meaning. On March 1, authorization for remaining in Haiti, the U.S. military forces, terminates.

There may be some who choose to debate that legally. But it is impossible for me to concede that, absent further authorization, that the President would violate the will of this Congress in remaining.

After February 1, on an expedited basis, members of this institution can go to the floor to specifically direct the President to remove the U.S. Armed Forces.

There may be well reasoned legal arguments constitutionally on all sides as to the powers involved. But I do not believe that the Clinton administration would violate the expressed will of this institution.

I believe that when the Congress speaks on this issue that we will proceed together. And notwithstanding the legal judgments that were provided by Secretary Sherman, I believe that the President of the United States has enough respect for this institution, and recognizes the necessity of this government remaining united in the matter of foreign policy, that when either in response to Mr. Hastings' motions, or Mr. Gilman's, or my own that the judgment of this House will prevail.

SUPPORT FOR OPEN RULE

Mr. BURTON. Would the gentleman yield for a question, please, my good friend?

Mr. TORRICELLI. I would be happy to yield.

Mr. BURTON. Since you are the sponsor of the resolution, and since it will be brought to the floor undoubtedly, would you be in opposition to having an open rule, so that we can have a full and thorough debate, and propose amendments to make the resolution better for all concerned?

Mr. TORRICELLI. As the gentleman knows, of course that is not my judgment. It is my own belief that the rule should be as open or as open as possible to allow for a free, fair, and open debate. The commitment that I believe that we have to date is simply one to allow a minority position and to allow Mr. Hastings' position. I personally do not have opposition going beyond that. But I am not sure that my view is really relevant.

Mr. BURTON. I appreciate the sponsor saying that we should have an open rule. Thank you.

Chairman HAMILTON. Is there further discussion?

VOTE ON H.J. RES. 416

Mr. GILMAN. Mr. Chairman, I move the resolution.

Chairman HAMILTON. The question occurs on H.J. Res. 416.

All those in favor signify by saying aye.

Those opposed no.

In the opinion of the chair, the ayes have it.

Mr. GILMAN. Mr. Chairman.

Chairman HAMILTON. The gentleman from New York.

Mr. GILMAN. Mr. Chairman, on that I would call for a roll call.

Chairman HAMILTON. All those in favor of taking the vote by roll call raise their hands.

The Clerk will call the roll.

Mr. VAN DUSEN. Mr. Hamilton.

Chairman HAMILTON. Aye.

Mr. VAN DUSEN. Mr. Gejdenson.
Mr. GEJDENSON. Aye.
Mr. VAN DUSEN. Mr. Lantos.
Mr. LANTOS. Aye.
Mr. VAN DUSEN. Mr. Torricelli.
Mr. TORRICELLI. Aye.
Mr. VAN DUSEN. Mr. Berman.
Mr. BERMAN. Aye.
Mr. VAN DUSEN. Mr. Ackerman.
Mr. ACKERMAN. Aye.
Mr. VAN DUSEN. Mr. Johnston.
Mr. JOHNSTON. Aye.
Mr. VAN DUSEN. Mr. Engel.
Mr. ENGEL. Aye.
Mr. VAN DUSEN. Mr. Faleomavaega.
Mr. FALEOMAVAEGA. Aye.
Mr. VAN DUSEN. Mr. Oberstar.
Chairman HAMILTON. Aye by proxy.
Mr. VAN DUSEN. Mr. Schumer.
Chairman HAMILTON. Aye by proxy.
Mr. VAN DUSEN. Mr. Martinez.
Mr. MARTINEZ. Aye.
Mr. VAN DUSEN. Mr. Borski.
[No response.]
Mr. VAN DUSEN. Mr. Payne.
Mr. PAYNE. Although I oppose it, I will vote aye in order to bring it to the floor.
Mr. VAN DUSEN. Mr. Andrews.
Mr. ANDREWS. Aye.
Mr. VAN DUSEN. Mr. Menendez.
Mr. MENENDEZ. Aye.
Mr. VAN DUSEN. Mr. Brown.
[No response.]
Mr. VAN DUSEN. Ms. McKinney.
Ms. McKinney. Aye.
Mr. VAN DUSEN. Ms. Cantwell.
Ms. CANTWELL. Aye.
Mr. VAN DUSEN. Aye.
Mr. VAN DUSEN. Mr. Hastings.
Mr. HASTINGS. Aye.
Mr. VAN DUSEN. Mr. Fingerhut.
Mr. FINGERHUT. Aye.
Mr. VAN DUSEN. Mr. Deutsch.
Mr. DEUTSCH. Aye.
Mr. VAN DUSEN. Mr. Wynn.
Mr. WYNN. Aye.
Mr. VAN DUSEN. Mr. Edwards.
Chairman HAMILTON. Aye by proxy.
Mr. VAN DUSEN. Mr. McCloskey.
Mr. MCCLOSKEY. Aye.
Mr. VAN DUSEN. Mr. Sawyer.
Mr. SAWYER. Aye.
Mr. VAN DUSEN. Mr. Gutierrez.
Chairman HAMILTON. Aye by proxy.

Mr. VAN DUSEN. Mr. Gilman.
Mr. GILMAN. No.
Mr. VAN DUSEN. Mr. Goodling.
Mr. GILMAN. No by proxy.
Mr. VAN DUSEN. Mr. Leach.
Mr. LEACH. No.
Mr. VAN DUSEN. Mr. Roth.
Mr. GILMAN. No by proxy.
Mr. VAN DUSEN. Ms. Snowe.
Ms. SNOWE. No.
Mr. VAN DUSEN. Mr. Hyde.
Mr. GILMAN. No by proxy.
Mr. VAN DUSEN. Mr. Bereuter.
Mr. GILMAN. No by proxy.
Mr. VAN DUSEN. Mr. Smith.
Mr. SMITH. No.
Mr. VAN DUSEN. Mr. Burton.
Mr. BURTON. No.
Mr. VAN DUSEN. Mrs. Meyers.
Mrs. MEYERS. No.
Mr. VAN DUSEN. Mr. Gallegly.
Mr. GILMAN. No by proxy.
Mr. VAN DUSEN. Ms. Ros-Lehtinen.
Ms. ROS-LEHTINEN. No.
Mr. VAN DUSEN. Mr. Ballenger.
Mr. BALLENGER. No.
Mr. VAN DUSEN. Mr. Rohrabacher.
Mr. ROHRABACHER. No.
Mr. VAN DUSEN. Mr. Levy.
Mr. GILMAN. No by proxy.
Mr. VAN DUSEN. Mr. Manzullo.
Mr. MANZULLO. No.
Mr. VAN DUSEN. Mr. Diaz-Balart.
Mr. DIAZ-BALART. No.
Mr. VAN DUSEN. Mr. Royce.
Mr. ROYCE. No.
Mr. VAN DUSEN. Mr. Borski.
Mr. BORSKI. Aye.
Mr. VAN DUSEN. Mr. Brown.
Chairman HAMILTON. Aye by proxy.

Mr. VAN DUSEN. On this vote, Mr. Chairman, there are 27 ayes and 18 nays.

Chairman HAMILTON. The resolution is approved.

Mr. GILMAN. Mr. Chairman, I request that the minority have the customary 3 days in order to file its views on this matter.

Chairman HAMILTON. Without objection, so ordered.

Mr. GILMAN. Thank you.

Chairman HAMILTON. The committee stands adjourned.

[Whereupon, at 12:51 p.m., the committee was adjourned.]

APPENDIX 1

103D CONGRESS
2D SESSION

H. J. RES. 416

Providing limited authorization for the participation of United States Armed Forces in the multinational force in Haiti and providing for the prompt withdrawal of United States Armed Forces from Haiti.

IN THE HOUSE OF REPRESENTATIVES

SEPTEMBER 28, 1994

Mr. TORRICELLI (for himself and Mr. HAMILTON) introduced the following joint resolution; which was referred jointly to the Committees on Foreign Affairs and Rules

JOINT RESOLUTION

Providing limited authorization for the participation of United States Armed Forces in the multinational force in Haiti and providing for the prompt withdrawal of United States Armed Forces from Haiti.

Resolved by the Senate and House of Representatives of the United States of America in Congress assembled,

SECTION 1. SHORT TITLE.

This joint resolution may be cited as the "Limited Authorization for the United States-led Force in Haiti Resolution".

SEC. 2. FINDINGS AND STATEMENT OF POLICY.

(a) FINDINGS.—The Congress finds the following:

(1) On September 18, 1994, the special delegation to Haiti succeeded in convincing the de facto authorities in Haiti to sign the Port-au-Prince Agreement under which such authorities agreed to leave power.

(2) On September 18, 1994, after the Port-au-Prince Agreement was reached, the President ordered the deployment of United States Armed Forces in and around Haiti.

(3) On September 21, 1994, the President submitted a report, consistent with the War Powers Resolution (50 U.S.C. 1541 et seq.), on the introduction of United States Armed Forces into Haiti.

(4) The Congress fully supports the men and women of the United States Armed Forces who are carrying out their mission in Haiti with professional excellence and dedicated patriotism.

(b) STATEMENT OF POLICY.—The Congress declares the following:

(1) The United States-led force in Haiti should use all necessary means to protect United States citizens, to stabilize the security situation in Haiti so that orderly progress may be made in transferring the functions of government in that country to the

democratically-elected government of Haiti, and to facilitate the provision of humanitarian assistance to the people of Haiti.

(2) Transfer of operations in Haiti from the United States-led force in Haiti to the United Nations-led force in Haiti should be facilitated and expedited to the fullest extent possible.

(3) United States Armed Forces should be withdrawn from Haiti as soon as possible.

SEC. 3. AUTHORIZATION FOR USE OF UNITED STATES ARMED FORCES.

(a) AUTHORIZATION.—Subject to subsection (b), United States Armed Forces are authorized to participate in the United States-led force in Haiti only—

(1) to protect United States citizens;

(2) to stabilize the security situation in Haiti so that orderly progress may be made in transferring the functions of government in that country to the democratically-elected government of Haiti; and

(3) to facilitate the provision of humanitarian assistance to the people of Haiti.

(b) LIMITATIONS.—

(1) TERMINATION OF AUTHORIZATION.—The authorization provided by subsection (a) shall expire on March 1, 1995.

(2) PROHIBITION ON FOREIGN COMMAND.—United States Armed Forces described in subsection (a) shall remain under the command and control of officers of the United States Armed Forces at all times.

SEC. 4. REPORTS TO CONGRESS.

(a) IN GENERAL.—The President shall submit to the Congress reports on—

(1) the participation of United States Armed Forces in the United States-led force in Haiti and the United Nations-led force in Haiti, including—

(A) the number of members of the United States Armed Forces that are participating in such United States-led force and such United Nations-led force;

(B) the functions of such Armed Forces; and

(C) the costs of deployment of such Armed Forces; and

(2) the efforts to withdraw United States Armed Forces from Haiti, including—

(A) for the purpose of achieving a transition from the United States-led force in Haiti to the United Nations-led force in Haiti, the status of efforts to implement the Port-au-

Prince Agreement and to otherwise carry out the terms of United Nations Security Council Resolutions 917 (May 6, 1994) and 940 (July 31, 1994);

(B) the status of plans to accomplish such transition to the United Nations-led force in Haiti; and

(C) the status of plans to withdraw United States Armed Forces from Haiti.

(b) REPORTING DATES.—A report under this section shall be submitted—

(1) not later than November 30, 1994, covering the period since September 18, 1994;

(2) not later than December 31, 1994, covering the period since the report described in paragraph (1); and

(3) not later than February 1, 1995, covering the period since the report described in paragraph (2).

(c) WAR POWERS RESOLUTION REPORTING REQUIREMENTS.—The requirements of this section do not supersede the requirements of the War Powers Resolution (50 U.S.C. 1541 et seq.).

SEC. 5. REASSEMBLY OF CONGRESS.

It is the sense of the Congress that the speaker of the House of Representatives and the majority leader of the Senate, acting jointly after consultation with the minority leader of the House of Representatives and the minority leader of the Senate, respectively, should monitor closely events in Haiti in considering whether to exercise any authority that may be granted to reassemble the Congress after the adjournment of the Congress sine die, if the public interest shall warrant it.

SEC. 6. JOINT RESOLUTION PROHIBITING CONTINUED USE OF UNITED STATES ARMED FORCES IN HAITI.

(a) IN GENERAL.—If a joint resolution described in subsection (b) is enacted, the President shall remove United States Armed Forces from Haiti in accordance with such joint resolution.

(b) DESCRIPTION OF JOINT RESOLUTION.—For purposes of subsection (a), a joint resolution described in this subsection is a joint resolution the matter after the resolving clause of which is as follows: "Pursuant to section 6 of the Limited Authorization for the United States-led Force in Haiti Resolution, the Congress hereby directs the President to remove United States Armed Forces from Haiti not later than 30 days after the date of the enactment of this joint resolution, except for a limited number of members of the United States Armed Forces sufficient to protect United States diplomatic facilities and personnel.''.

(c) PRIORITY PROCEDURES.—

(1) INTRODUCTION OF JOINT RESOLUTION.—Paragraph (2) shall only apply to a joint resolution described in subsection (b) and introduced on or after the date on which the President submits, or is required to submit, the report required by section 4(b)(3).

(2) CONSIDERATION OF JOINT RESOLUTION.—Only one joint resolution described in subsection (b) and introduced in accordance with paragraph (1) shall be considered in accordance with the procedures described in section 7 of the War Powers Resolution (50 U.S.C. 1546), except that, for purposes of such consideration, the term "calendar days" in such section shall be deemed to mean "legislative days".

SEC. 7. DEFINITIONS.

For purposes of this joint resolution, the following definitions apply:

(1) LEGISLATIVE DAYS.—The term "legislative days" means days in which the House of Representatives is in session.

(2) PORT-AU-PRINCE AGREEMENT.—The term "Port-au-Prince Agreement" means the agreement reached between the United States special delegation and the de facto authorities in Haiti on September 18, 1994.

(3) UNITED NATIONS-LED FORCE IN HAITI.—The term "United Nations-led force in Haiti" means the United Nations Mission in Haiti (commonly referred to as "UNMIH") authorized by United Nations Security Council Resolutions 867 (September 23, 1993), 905 (March 23, 1994), 933 (June 30, 1994), and 940 (July 31, 1994).

(4) UNITED STATES-LED FORCE IN HAITI.—The term "United States-led force in Haiti" means the multinational force (commonly referred to as "MNF") authorized by United Nations Security Council Resolution 940 (July 31, 1994).

THE DEPUTY SECRETARY OF DEFENSE

WASHINGTON, D.C. 20301

29 SEP 1994

Honorable Lee H. Hamilton
Chairman
Committee on Foreign Affairs
House of Representatives
Washington, D.C. 20515

Dear Mr. Chairman:

During my September 28 congressional testimony, you requested additional information on the total costs that are being incurred by the US Government to support our relief effort in Haiti. Enclosure 1 is OMB's response to Senator Byrd on these costs and enclosure 2 is a fact sheet which summarizes and simplifies the letter OMB prepared for Senator Byrd. In both cases, the figures include the estimated costs of all government agencies.

Sincerely,

Enclosures

cc: Honorable Benjamin A. Gilman
Ranking Republican

APPENDIX 2

EXECUTIVE OFFICE OF THE PRESIDENT
OFFICE OF MANAGEMENT AND BUDGET
WASHINGTON, D.C. 20503

THE DIRECTOR

SEP 27 1994

Honorable Robert C. Byrd
Chairman
Committee on Appropriations
United States Senate
Washington, D.C. 20510-6025

Dear Mr. Chairman:

Thank you for your recent letter regarding the cost of U.S. operations in Haiti. Let me assure you that I share your interest in identifying, as quickly and accurately as possible, the costs the Federal government is likely to incur in and around Haiti.

The agreement reached on September 18th between the U.S. delegation and the de facto government of Haiti has significantly changed some of the planning factors that had previously been used to determine the cost of U.S. Haiti-related operations. We are assessing the impact of these changes and will not be able to provide final cost estimates until some of the key factors have been decided. In the meantime, however, we have provided below, preliminary estimates of costs for FY 1994, 1995 and 1996, where available, for the following operations:

- Migration Operation, covering interdiction, immigration processing and safe haven construction and operating activities by, primarily, the Departments of Defense and State and the U.S. Coast Guard.

- Sanctions Enforcement Operation, covering enhancing the capabilities of the Dominican Republic border patrol and supporting personnel who monitor sanctions enforcement at the border. It also includes the U.S. naval sanctions enforcement at sea.

- Peacekeeping Operation, covering the U.S.-led Multi-National Force (MNF) and the U.N. peacekeeping mission in Haiti (UNMIH) to restore Haiti's democratic government.

- Reconstruction Assistance, covering humanitarian aid and economic/social/political reconstruction, including the reconstitution of Haitian police and military. This assistance will be carried out primarily by the U.S. Agency for International Development (USAID) and the Departments of State and Justice.

Enclosure 1

Fiscal Year 1994 Costs

The majority of FY 1994 incremental costs are associated with the migration and sanctions enforcement operations (estimated at roughly $200 million, including funds for the U.S. Coast Guard and the U.S. naval enforcement of sanctions at sea) and the early phases of the MNF. Our costs for the MNF; which began September 19th, are still under review because the size, operating tempo and timing could all be affected by the changed circumstances of its arrival. With respect to reconstruction assistance, it should be noted that USAID has been carrying out a program of assistance in Haiti, overwhelmingly humanitarian in nature, throughout FY 1994. The program has been implemented solely through non-governmental agencies. The total cost of that program during this fiscal year, including incremental costs, is estimated at about $95 million, most of which had been budgeted for earlier in the year.

Some of the FY 1994 incremental costs, i.e., $48 million for naval sanctions enforcement, were covered by a previously enacted supplemental appropriation. Other FY 1994 incremental costs will be covered through diversion of funds from other operational activities, reprogramming of available funds, the drawdown of available DoD services and stocks, and the use of other authorities.

Fiscal Year 1995/96 Costs

For Fiscal Year 1995, the costs of the migrant operation and the sanctions enforcement operation are likely to be negligible. The majority of FY 1995 incremental costs are associated with the peacekeeping operation -- the MNF and UNMIH -- and Department of State and USAID reconstruction assistance. As we noted in paragraph 6 of our recent report to you in response to section 8147 (c) of the DoD Appropriations Act of 1994, a preliminary estimate of the U.S. deployment-related costs associated with the MNF and UNMIH through FY 1996 was projected at $500-$600 million. This estimate is likely to change for the reasons cited above and because the timing of a transition from the MNF to UNMIH, currently uncertain, is a key determinant of cost. We will provide you with more detailed estimates as they become available.

Under reconstruction assistance, humanitarian aid will continue in FY 1995 and will be augmented by reconstruction activities. Total reconstruction assistance in FY 1995, including restructuring of the Haitian police and military, could be around $200 million. There is no firm estimate yet for FY 1996 reconstruction assistance.

Some FY 1995 incremental costs for Haiti activities can be covered within available resources as in FY 1994, but consideration will be given to submission of an FY 1995 supplemental when better information on actual costs is available either in February with the 1996 budget or later in the year. We anticipate working with the Congress to identify the most appropriate designation for a potential supplemental request under the Balanced Budget and Emergency Deficit Control Act of 1985.

APPENDIX 3

2 8 SEP 1994

Honorable Thomas S. Foley
Speaker
House of Representatives
Washington, D.C. 20515-6501

Dear Mr. Speaker:

We are writing to express our opposition to any legislation that would require U.S. military operations in Haiti to end on a fixed date.

We have developed a phased plan that encompasses the introduction of U.S. forces, establishment of public order, gradual reduction in U.S. force level, transition to a U.N. mission, and withdrawal of U.S. troops. According to this plan, the initial phase of predominant American involvement will end in a matter of months, and the UNMIH phase will end with the inauguration of a new, democratically elected President of Haiti in early 1996.

However, it is too early in the operation to set fixed dates. For the operation to succeed and meet the intended schedule with minimum risk to U.S. personnel, our military forces need to proceed with achieving objectives, not meeting fixed deadlines. The success of the operation to date is due largely to the force commander having the freedom both to devise and implement military plans and to make necessary adjustments as circumstances change on the ground. A fixed end date would deprive us of this advantage.

More important, a legislatively required withdrawal date would change the dynamic on the ground and affect the actions of our friends and those who oppose us. Those who oppose us will find reasons to try to outlast us. Our friends -- including those who would support us in the MNF and those who would relieve us in UNMIH -- might find excuses not to join us. Also, if Congress were to direct a withdrawal from Haiti now, our troops would lose an important psychological advantage they now enjoy. The bottom line is that the dynamic created by a mandated withdrawal date could make the situation more dangerous to our troops.

Sincerely,

John M. Shalikashvili
Chairman
of the Joint Chiefs of Staff

William J. Perry
Secretary of Defense

In your letter, you requested that we identify the participation, financial or otherwise, undertaken by other nations. We are not asking other countries to fund the costs of U.S. military operations. Member countries of the Organization for Economic Cooperation and Development (OECD) participating in the MNF will cover their own costs. The U.S. will cover the incremental costs of participation by non-OECD countries. When the UNMIH force takes over, the peacekeeping operation will be funded through the U.N. As you point out, the U.S. is assessed just over 30 percent of the costs of U.N. peacekeeping operations. With respect to economic reconstruction, the international community has been centrally involved in drawing up a comprehensive, multi-year economic assistance program for Haiti. We anticipate significant international participation in this program.

Thank you again for your letter. Please be assured that we will continue to provide you additional information as estimates become available.

Sincerely,

Alice M. Rivlin
Acting Director

USG Estimated Costs of Haiti Operations
($ in Millions)

As a result of the agreement reached on September 18 between the US delegation and the de facto government of Haiti, many of the planning factors which determine the cost of the US Haiti operation have changed. We are currently updating these changes and will not be able to provide final cost estimates until some of the key factors have been decided. In the meantime, provided below are preliminary estimates for FYs 1994-1996 of migrant operations, sanctions enforcement, and peacekeeping operations based on current information available.

Migrant Operations/Sanctions Enforcement 200

Covers costs related to interdiction, immigration processing, safe haven construction activities, US naval sanctions enforcement at sea, and the multinational observer group that is monitoring enforcement at the Dominican Republic/Haiti border primarily incurred by the Departments of Defense and State and the US Coast Guard. FY 1995 costs are likely to be negligible.

Peacekeeping Operations 500 - 600

A preliminary estimate of the US deployment-related costs associated with the Multinational Force (MNF) and the UN Mission in Haiti (UNMIH), through FY 1996 was projected at $500-600 million. The costs for the MNF, which began September 19, are still under review because the size, operating tempo and timing could all be affected by the changed circumstances of its arrival. This estimate is also likely to change due to the uncertainty of the transition from the MNF to UNMIH, which is a key determinant of cost. The above estimate also includes Department of State costs for the UN assessment and other support costs related to both the MNF and UNMIH.

Reconstruction Assistance 295

The USAID has been carrying out a program of assistance in Haiti, overwhelmingly humanitarian in nature, throughout FY 1994. The total FY 1994 cost of that program is estimated at $95 million. Total reconstruction assistance in FY 1995, including restructuring the Haitian police and military was estimated to be around $200 million. There is no firm estimate yet for FY 1996 reconstruction assistance.

Enclosure 2

APEX
TP
9780160462269
76901945-68